Hidden Debts

A Memoir from Italy

by

MARTIN ATTWOOD

iUniverse, Inc.
New York Bloomington

iUniverse books may be ordered through booksellers or by contacting:

iUniverse
1663 Liberty Drive
Bloomington, IN 47403
www.iuniverse.com
1-800-Authors (1-800-288-4677)

ISBN: 978-1-4401-3833-1 (sc)
ISBN: 978-1-4401-3834-8 (ebook)

Printed in the United States of America

iUniverse rev. date: 6/16/2009

Front cover illustration

Madonna della Misericordia
Pietro di Domenico da Montepulciano 1420 (circa)
Tempera on poplar wood
54 x 43 cms
Musée du Petit Palais Avignon

Martin Attwood was born in Britain and grew up in Kenya. He lived in Italy for over thirty years where, amongst other things, he was a farmer, a school teacher and a lecturer for AHI International. 'Before the Palio', his first memoir was republished in 2003 as 'Fishing with Amedeo and other histories'. He has a married daughter and recently became a grandfather.

The author is extremely grateful to Lyn Baines, Jessica Collins, Fredrick Munc and everyone at Moulin du Mas de Vaudoret for all their help.

"Debt - who owes what to whom, or to what, and how that debt gets paid - is a subject much larger than money. It has to do with our basic sense of fairness, a sense that is embedded in all of our exchanges with our fellow human beings."

Margaret Atwood
Life & Debt, New York Times, 21.10.08

For the sake of privacy almost all the names of characters in this book have been changed.

for if

Prologue

The Lady stands centre stage facing front. We see her from head to toe. She seems, on the whole, to be about thirty years old, more or less. Youngish anyway. She stares out at us directly with a bland expression, bored even, like she's been standing there for ages waiting for something to happen, to break the spell. But nothing ever does happen, or so it seems. Perhaps she has a sense of foreboding, an awareness of a tragedy yet to happen.

Mostly she stands upright as if being measured by one of those vertical rulers, her height being noted down on some medical or official document. Sometimes she takes a break and rests her weight on one leg letting the other bend slightly at the knee to ease her blood circulation. When she does that we can see the shape of her knee and lower thigh through the folds of her garment.

Her arms are outstretched and she holds out her cloak with both hands. In winter, the inside of her cloak is lined with rectangles of white ermine fur, insulation to retain her body heat. In other seasons the inside of her cloak isn't always the traditional blue we know she almost always wears elsewhere. Blue is her colour; the most expensive pigment or dye, made from lapis lazuli mined in present day Afghanistan which had been exchanged again and again, rising in price in markets as it travelled west across caravan routes until it reached the Black Sea where Venetian and Genoan traders, picked up their precious cargo and shipped it to Italy where it was eventually crushed into a fine powder to make ultra marine, blue from over the seas. She rarely wears the red dress we normally associate under her blue cloak. Red, like the blue, was more expensive than gold, and was made by crushing the dried corpses of the female cochineal insect which were picked off the holm oaks, their feeding ground, just before they laid their eggs in June. Dried and crushed, they were ground into that deep red pigment.

This lady is dressed in all colours and patterns depending on the whim of painters and patrons. Could be she wears a gold cloak with a latticed fabric gown, or a green cloak over a yellow dress. The permutations are unlimited.

She lets go of her cloak only when someone from Up There plonks a chubby kicker with the expression of a thirty-something-year-old who looks like he can see around corners into her arms. Then a couple of angels take over and hold out her cloak.

The lady seems oblivious to the dramas unfolding

underneath her sheltering cloak, for down there, in her personal sanctuary, are the little people.

The little people stand or kneel depending. They may be just a couple, a man on one side, a woman, more often the man's wife, on the other. They may be a small intimate group of eight or sixteen perhaps. Or there may be a crowd down there jostling for a view out from under the shelter of her protection. Sometimes the women are all on one side and the men on the other. Other times there may be only men. In one rare instance there are only women and in some examples, everyone, men and women, rich and poor, noble and humble, are mixed up together.

The little people range from kings and queens, popes, cardinals, bishops, monks, abbots, nuns, abbesses, parish priests, stern municipal officials, middle class burgers, patrons of the arts, merchants, bankers, tradespeople, housewives, poor people, even newly wed couples. Sometimes there are the hooded members of religious orders, anonymous penitents with holes cut into the backs of their white gowns so they can lash their flesh to a bloody pulp leaving what at first glance look like Neapolitan pizzas pinned to their backs. In rare instances we can see portraits of the artists themselves, their signatures or tags in a mainly illiterate society.

Most of the little people gaze up at their protectress in awe, sometimes with hands in supplication. A few gaze out into the space behind us, the viewers, like the Astrid look-alike in the church of San Pietro in Tuscania. Occasionally, groups of wealthy courtiers will virtually ignore their protectress as they back-bite bitchily and in-fight fractiously amongst themselves within the shelter of her protection and patronage. Courtiers tend to do this.

The one uniting bond between this varied cross-section of medieval society bubbling away beneath her cloak is Her. The Lady herself. The Protectress.

She is the *Madonna della Misericordia,* the Madonna of Mercy.

She is the patroness of hospitals, charities and the justice, or she was, long ago. It's to her I'm turning for help. It's the justice bit that I'm tapping into. I'm up to my neck in legal shit in Machiavelliland and it's not looking good. I don't even tell my lawyer Michelangela, who said we need to go into court with all our weapons ready even if we don't have to use them. This Lady is my secret weapon. I need her help. She's my trump card, so I keep her hidden up my sleeve.

1

Tigerlily's Warning

It's a Saturday morning.

It's Saturday, September 8th in the year of our great and good Laird, the all-powerful, all seeing, all knowing landowner, 2001.

It's market day on a Saturday morning in Orvieto, as it is in just about any other town in central Italy or the world.

Saturdays are also my lecture days. So are Mondays. I lecture on Italian history through its art and architecture. My brief, when I received it, was to talk about the Etruscans, medieval Italian art and the Renaissance. My daughter pointed out the medieval bit. That added half a millennium to my time span. If you're going to talk about the Etruscans and medieval Italian art history then there's the small matter of one thousand years of the Romans to ignore at your peril. As anyone knows, or should know, you can't talk about

Italian history without including the Romans. You can hardly talk about any history without referring to the Romans. That goes for medicine, law, linguistics and a host of other subjects. If you include the Romans then you can't ignore the hangover after their party came to an end, the so called Dark Ages. So my lectures span two thousand five hundred years in the space of two and a half hours. I talk at the speed of one thousand years an hour which has to be something of a record.

I enjoy my lectures. The people who listen to them seem to like them too if the applause is anything to go by.

I lecture in Cortona in Tuscany to mainly Americans, mostly retired, from careers as varied as pathology to economics, so I get feedback ranging from "That's the exact colour of a three day old corpse" while I'm standing in front of a Deposition of Christ by Luca Signorelli in the Uffizi gallery in Florence, with a retired mortician from Chicago and his wife. Or "Hyper-inflation in the mid-third century of the Roman empire forced many citizens to decide to become slaves as slavery was seen as a fiscal refuge from the punitive taxes in kind." That was a Roman historian and I'm teaching his grandmother to suck eggs.

The Saturday market in Orvieto is held in the *Piazza del Popolo* in front of the *Palazzo del Capitano del Popolo,* the palace of the Captain of the People. This was the medieval title of an outsider, a non-Orvietan, who arbitrated in internal disputes having no vested interests locally. He was appointed by the priors of the town and was usually contracted for a two year term during which he was forbidden to socialise with the locals being under a form of palace arrest. Venetians, with their long history of diplomacy, were favoured captains of the people.

In Orvieto's annual procession of the feast of the cloth (the sacred bloodstained altarcloth on which a Bohemian priest during mass in the church of Santa Cristina in Bolsena in 1262, accidentally spilt the wine which was said to have turned to blood) the role of the *Capitano del Popolo* is played by a man called Sergio. He's very tall and upright, elegantly elderly with long, flowing silver hair and beard and his moustache protrudes beyond his ears. As the procession sets off from where they sell umbrellas, shoes, handbags, underwear and sunglasses on Saturdays, Sergio descends the wide, external staircase of the palace dressed in his middle-aged outfit, a glittering breast plate, and carrying his helmet under his left arm. He joins the line of fancy dressed locals playing members of the thirty something major and minor guilds that once ran the business community in the town, with their banners, drums and trumpets as they set off in their medieval colourful costumes for the magnificent cathedral where the altar cloth is removed from its reliquary and paraded around the town. The whole circus of the costumed crowd that includes children, nuns and friars is brought up by four handicapped men in their electric wheelchairs. The day after the procession, usually held in May, Sergio gets his beard trimmed and his hair cut.

I don't do the market this Saturday as I don't need

any plastic bags containing vegetables, frying pans or underpants. I buy yesterday's Guardian newspaper dated Friday September 7th 2001 from Paolo's news agency just beneath the clock tower, the tallest of Orvieto's remaining medieval towers, just down the narrow street from the market. If you ask Paolo for a Guardian for the first time he'll ask "Which do you want: today's or yesterday's?" When you say "Today's", he'll say "Come back tomorrow".

I'll take the train from Orvieto to Camucia, the new town below the ancient city of Cortona.

A short walk from Camucia station is one of the best bars in Italy: Vanelli's. Bar Montanucci in Orvieto was once acclaimed the second best bar in Italy and ever since then they never let you forget it. Believe you me, Vanelli is much better than the second-best bar in Italy and they're all really nice, happy and polite people who work there. I've time for a quick 'light lunch' then on to the bus for the old city of Cortona up on the hill.

The bus, after winding up past olive groves braced with dry-stone walls and renaissance churches, drops me off in Piazza Garribaldi right outside Cortona. Francesco, a local loony, guides it in, shows the passengers off and generally gets in the way. He honestly believes it's his job. No one interferes. They just let him live his fantasy.

This is the route by which I came into Cortona for the first time almost twenty eight years earlier. My then wife and I had come to see a farm nearby that I'd read about on a real estate agent's list that I'd found by accident when I'd answered someone else's phone in an office in which I worked in London. Looking for a piece of paper to write a message on, I picked up an A4 sheet headed 'Houses in Tuscany, Cortona'. I hadn't meant to answer that phone but changed my mind and changed my life.

On our first morning in Cortona, we'd looked at a farm on the list that was down in the valley below the hill town. That evening I'd found another farm, up in the hills behind Cortona, a much better deal and location and we'd bought that without a penny to our names. An English pal's father's stepmother, also the first wife's sister, (yes, it's complicated) had a friend an American novelist staying in the house of an English artist, who along with a generous mediator called Bruno and an extremely helpful local notary called Donatella (who spoke English), made it all possible. My brother, sister and I sold the cottage in England we'd inherited from our mother and went to live on that farm. My marriage didn't survive the move but I held out for over 20 years. I left the hill farm when things in Perugia got super-heated up in the aftermath of the trouble Astrid left in her wake. I went to live in Orvieto for my own safety.

So coming back to Cortona twice a week is like coming home. It used to be a slightly gloomy, dark and crumbling Tuscan hill town "populated by bookish foreigners" as a guide book put it. The town is twinned with Chateau Chinon in France where the once mayor, Francois Mitterand, went on to become president of France. He made regular visits to Cortona, sometimes un-announced. In 1987, he was flown in and spent a couple of days surprising tourists as he sat at a bar in piazza Signorelli. Before leaving, he visited Perugia and accompanied by two sunglazed bouncers and the mayor of the capital of Umbria, strolled down the Corso Vanucci. A French touring citizen spotted the president and rushed up to him saying something like

"Monsieur Le President, ow comb I vote for you for twenty ears yet I av to meet you een Perugia?"

The president coolly replied

"You should go more often to Cortona."

As the two hundredth anniversary of the French revolution loomed, the local authorities began to spiff up the town. The cobwebs of telephone wires that almost hid the sky from the street were bundled up and concentrated into a few discreet cables. Facades were replastered. Streets were repaved in the local sandstone flags. Cortona went upmarket. It was given a stratospheric boost when an American poet moved in, wrote a massive bestselling book about how she bought and restored a house near the town and estate agencies quickly replaced cobblers and tailors, art galleries took over where fruit and vegetable sellers and grocery stores had once been.

This is the town where I work.

I cross over the Piazza Garribaldi to the Albergo San Luca. This is the hotel where the American groups are housed and they're fed in Tonino's restaurant next door. The hotel is built on the edge of the hill so ground level is on the top floor and then you go down six floors.

The year we bought the farm, we came out at Christmas to sign the contract. Some friends of my wife's from London, a couple and their twin two-year-old daughters arrived before us and booked into the Albergo San Luca and were given a room on the third floor down. Their first night they put the twins to bed and went out for a meal, locking the door and taking the key with them. When they came back there was uproar on their floor. While they were out the twins had gotten out of their beds, gone into the bathroom and turned on the taps. The bath filled then overflowed. Water seeped down onto the floor below, then the floor below that before someone came upon the cascade. The staff couldn't find the room key so they called the cook who hacked his way through the door with a meat cleaver. They were clearing up the mess when the parents got back from their evening out.

We arrived the next day and I knew the San Luca was the most expensive hotel in Cortona so we checked into the Albergo Italia on the other side of town. The twins and their parents came with us, much to the relief of the staff at the San Luca.

One evening we all went out for a meal. The twins' parents locked them in their room thinking, as the bathroom was down the corridor, there wouldn't be any problems. When we got back they found the twins had painted a mural using their shit and eaten their mother's contraceptive pills. Two months later the mother was pregnant again and had another set of twins. The parents would have one more set of twins again making three pairs and they eventually become Quakers. I didn't know it at the time but the Albergo Italia was once the town brothel.

Today I go into reception where Mauro gives me a bottle of water and I ask how large the group is. The larger the better I think, as you get audience momentum once you've wound them up. Mauro tells me Natasia is running things this week.

The lecture room is on the second floor down, directly below the restaurant. One of the occupational hazards of this lectureship is the noise of waiters moving tables and chairs around on the floor above.

When I've put the slide cassette into the projector, checked the focus on the first slide and made adjustments, the first of the group trail in from their lunch. Just before the 2.30 scheduled start Natasia waltzes in. She's wearing a long black dress and looking gorgeous as usual. I've known her since she was three years old when I was in business with her father. He's German and her mother is Italian. Her grandmother is Russian. It's an interesting mix.

When the group are all in and sitting quietly talking, Natasia begins:

"Good afternoon everybody. I'd like to introduce Martin Attwood. He's British by birth, grew up in Kenya, worked for the Fine Arts Department of the British Council in London before moving to a farm in the hills above Cortona twenty five years ago. Five years ago he moved to Orvieto. This afternoon he'll be talking about the Etruscans. Afterwards Louise, your guide, will take you around the Museum of the Etruscan Academy. Enjoy the lecture."

I thank Natasia and she goes off to have a fag on the terrace. The audience still has some jet lag swilling around with the wine they had for lunch, so, with the lights out, we have a perfect recipe for a siesta, but I'll do my best to keep most of them awake for most of the time. I begin by talking about saints: Cortona has three patron saints which is more than its fair share. Saint Michael Archangel, who presides over who's going to heaven and who isn't on the day of judgement, patron saint of the town up until the 25th of April 1262, the day the Cortonese regained their town from the bishop of Arezzo whose army captured it four years earlier.

April 25th being Saint Marc's day, the Cortonese retired Saint Michael and adopted Saint Marc instead, the saint they share with the city of Venice. You can see the symbol of Saint Marc, a lion, dotted around both Cortona and Venice, carrying a book, the gospel of the eponymous saint. In Venice the book is open with the words "Peace be unto you my beloved apostle" written in Latin clearly displayed. In Cortona the lion carries a closed book. I asked a former mayor of Cortona why one book was closed and the other open and he said that since Cortona is much, much older than Venice, they keep the book open as they still have a lot to learn. I asked a Venetian tour guide her version of the open and closed gospels and she said that the Cortona lion holds a closed book because in Cortona they can't read.

I'll talk a bit about local archaeological discoveries, the origins of the Etruscans, their rise to dominance in central Italy, bronze, iron and gold, writing, funerary rites, the Etruscans' decline and eventual absorption by the rising phenomenon of Rome. I end with a slide of the statue of Octavian Augustus Caesar, the first of the Roman emperors. Those still awake applaud and those asleep wake up at the sound of clapping.

Louise has arrived. She's the group's local Etruscan museum guide. I've known her since she was a teenager. I introduce her, bid my farewells as the group troops out, collect my slides, get the bus to the station and get the 4.35 train back to Orvieto. I'm home by 6 and sitting on my upper terrace amongst my wisteria plant and cascading geraniums drinking chilled white Orvieto Classico wine, watching the dying sunlight glittering across the tips of the triangular facade of the cathedral and going over Monday's lecture in my mind.

This lecture is hot. The group are wide awake and ready. I wind them up with a laugh:

"Good morning ladies and gentlemen. I hope you enjoyed your visits to Perugia and Assisi yesterday. I'm sure your guide explained what bitter enemies those two towns were back in the Middle Ages. They were constantly at each others' throats."

I don't mention my personal links with both towns otherwise the lecture will take all morning.

"This afternoon you go to Siena and on Tuesday it's Florence. If you think Perugia and Assisi were enemies, that's nothing compared to Siena and Florence. The Sienese have never forgiven Florence for besieging and capturing their city in the fifteen sixties when they came under Florentine control. That hatred is still alive and thriving today. To give you an example: a group of tourists was being taken around Siena by their guide and one of the group asked the guide if there was still rivalry today between Siena and Florence? The guide, without batting an eyelid, replied:

"In Siena, we try NOT to use the F-word."

That really cracks them up. Then I hit them with Romans, barbarians, popes, Holy Roman emperors, elves, goblins, heretics, domes, self-portraits and all that Renaissance stuff.

Sometimes, and it's rare, if I don't really warm to a group or they to me, I'll throw in something to shake them up like how in the late 12th century, a German Holy Roman Emperor married a Norman princess, kidnapped the King of England returning from a Crusade, and with the ransom money financed a campaign to recapture his wife's inheritance, the kingdom of Sicily, which his wife's cousin had usurped. The Emperor then staged a coronation: he had the usurper tied to a throne, and an iron crown was heated up red hot and nailed to the pretender's head.

I watch the winces ripple through the audience like a Mexican wave. It puts them right back up there on their toes.

I end up Monday's lecture with a particular bloodthirsty interpretation of Sandro Boticelli's magnificent painting 'The Allegory of Spring' in the Uffizi gallery in Florence. If I really like the group and they've laughed in all the right places and I can feel the electricity they've collectively generated as they hung onto every word, at this point I'll throw in a treat. Even if you, dear reader, never bought this book but borrowed it, or, dare I hope, stole it, I'm going to let you in on the treat too.

The Allegory of Spring contains, among its cast of vivid characters, one of the many versions of The Three Graces. They are three naked ladies in their sexual prime, standing with their arms entwined, the outside two facing us and the one in the middle facing the other way, or, the other way round depending on points of view. In this version Boticelli has clothed the three ladies in white, diaphanous gowns.

They are the three ancient Greek goddesses, Hera, Athena and Aphrodite. Hera is the wife of Zeus, the top god, who's always off having it off with other goddesses, demi-goddesses and humans, often disguised as an animal or a bird.

Understandably Hera is upset by all this unfaithfulness and stands to loose face among her peers in the Greek pantheon so, she and her two girlfriends, do everything in their power to put obstacles in the way of Zeus's philandering. This in turn irritates Zeus so he devises a way to split up the trio of ladies and he shrewdly plays on their vanity. He invents a beauty contest in which the contestants are the three goddesses. I like to think he calls it 'Miss Classical World'.

To judge the contest Zeus chooses Paris, the son of Priam king of Troy. Paris is well renowned in antiquity as having an eye for the ladies. The prize for the winner will be a golden apple from the garden of Hesperides.

After Paris eyes the girls once over, he gets back to Zeus and tells him to split the apple into three, as each of the contestants is as beautiful as the other.

"Go back and get me a winner" booms Zeus, not

wanting to be deprived of his fun, so Paris goes back and calls on the girls one by one.

First forward is Athena who offers Paris total dominion over the earth if he'll declare her the winner. Next comes Hera who tries to tempt Paris offering him all conquering power on earth.

Lastly comes Aphrodite who tells Paris if he thinks the three contestants are beautiful he ain't seen nothing yet. If Paris will award her the prize, she winks, she will introduce him to a lady besides whose beauty all others pale.

Well that does it! Paris awards Aphrodite the golden apple and exactly what Zeus intended happens, the three ladies start scratching out each others eyes in bitchiness.

But Aphrodite is true to her word. She introduces Paris to Helen, wife of Menelaus, king of Sparta and, incidentally, daughter of Zeus who earlier, disguised as a swan, had seduced Helen's mother Leda who got knocked up by her husband, an earlier Spartan king, later the same night. Leda gave birth by hatching an egg containing baby Helen and the twins Castor and Pollux, known to all Geminis.

On their first date, dinner for two, as Helen's hubby is away on business, Paris falls deeply in love with Helen and the couple elope to Troy and the rest, as they say, is mythology.

There are countless versions of The Three Graces going far back in antiquity and right through to the modern world. Greek and Roman versions abound. A Roman version stands on a plinth in the library off the aisle of Siena cathedral. The three naked ladies appear on Roman coins. They crop up in the late Middle Ages disguised as Faith, Hope and Charity but still only an excuse for painting naked ladies. Reubens gives them voluptuous flesh as was his way. Napoleon's favourite sculptor Canova made a copy of an earlier version of his that went for auction in New York recently for several million dollars. The French painter Robert Delauney, a contemporary of Picasso, painted a version around 1910 which included a view of the Eiffel tower. He called the painting 'The Judgement of Paris'. There are literally hundreds of versions throughout the history of western art. One of my lecture groups from McGill University in Canada told me of a version of The Three Graces by one of the Vanderbilt sisters who'd carved them as a fountain for the campus in the 1930's which the students had immediately renamed The Three Bares (sic).

When the laughter has died down I'll reinterpret Botticelli's Allegory of Spring in the light of a plot to murder Lorenzo di Medici in Florence cathedral in 1478, and, with the final flick to my coda, I'll reveal the sting in the tail. Then I'm done.

When the applause has died down I'll tell them where they can buy a copy of my book, Before the Palio, which is nearly out of print (but an agent in New York picked it up last month and wants to get it published properly) and at which bar I'll be at in town so they can bring me their copies and I'll sign and dedicate them.

I'm basking in the prospects ahead when the phone downstairs rings.

I don't rush down the polished terracotta steps

as I did two years ago, when I slipped, fell, and broke my back. I'm careful yet hasty enough not to want to miss the call.

I pick up the receiver.

"Hello?"

"Martin?"

"Hi Tigerlily. How are you?"

"Martin, sell everything! Everything you've got! Get out now!"

"Tigerlily, I can't sell everything just like that. I've got a judicial mortgage on the farm. It's going to take months to clear it and sell the place."

"Martin, don't say I never warned you. You'll remember this phone call for the rest of your life."

2

The getaway car

"How did you know they were going to do that?"

This was some months later. I was at the house, their Shangri-La in the next valley north from Cortona. It belongs to Edward, an elderly, pukka Englishman, who lives most of the year in Singapore. Tigerlily is his companion. Edward, though past official retirement age, is an extremely active and successful lawyer. Tigerlily is Chinese, almost half his age, and a compulsive and extremely successful gambler. Her idea of paradise is to sit down with three friends and play mahjong for serious stakes.

"I didn't" said Tigerlily "or rather we didn't."

"Who's we?" I asked.

"When you work in the money markets, you're watching those monitors 24/7. When you take a break someone else takes over. When that Leeson guy in

Hongkong started to come onto our radar we all watched him. Either he knew something we didn't or he was crazy. Turned out to be the latter and he took down Britain's oldest bank with him. In this case, we knew something enormous was going to happen and roughly when. We didn't know what or where."

I thought about this as the world order changed beyond recognition. Bang went any possible book deal. Worth as much as two of those pieces of paper fluttering down Canal Street with a horizontal mushroom cloud racing up behind them. It's books about firemen publishers want from now on. I haven't got a hope as I write about lighting fires, not putting them out.

If you have nineteen men, twenty originally, and get them fired up on the plan, put them through rigorous training, four through civilian airline pilot operating programmes, finance it all, check airline schedules down to the last detail, book hotels, tickets, everything, you're talking about a huge operation. How can all the people involved, from the top echelons of the organization, down through the financers, the planners, the trainers, the hit teams themselves, over what must have taken months of work; be expected not to let a little kitty out of the bag here and there? Word would have spread. Those little kitties would have gone forth and multiplied and, sooner or later, got to the ears of those guys who sit and watch for anything likely to indicate a minute shift, a breath of a breeze of change, any slight readjustment of tectonic plates in the geology of money. Suddenly they get wind of an earthquake, a tsunami, a catastrophe of unprecedented proportions. What do they do? Bale out and call around their families and friends and warn them of the impending disaster. Just as Barings Bank collapsed, so just about everything else came crashing down that Tuesday after Tigerlily's phone call.

Then there were those idiotic conspiracy theories. Some said no Jews went to work in the World Trade Centre that day. Read through the death toll list. Others said the US government planted explosives in the buildings. Like Dubya is that smart? I even heard that the closing shot of the distant twin towers in the movie 'Munich' directed by Stephen Spielberg about Mosad's assassination of the Black September assassins after the 1972 Olympics gave Al Quaida the idea for their target. Come on! Oh, Sam Bladen does movies?

If you really want to do the conspiracy theory thing, go back to when America was last ambushed. Where were all the US Pacific Fleet aircraft carriers when the Japanese hit Pearl Harbour?

Westerners still can't accept that a bunch of Arabs could organize and pull off such a stunt. Even most Arabs think it was an inside job. They don't believe they were capable of doing it. My best friend Ellie said that it was carried out with Swiss precision and I asked her if the Swiss would ever have had the imagination to even conceive of such a thing? When the site of the catastrophe was named Ground Zero, did those Christians who christened it forget who invented the zero?

Conspiracy theories, the patch of the partially

blind, the beat of the desperately bored, inevitably lead to the big question:

"What if ...?"

What if the theorists were right and there was a conspiracy to assassinate JFK? What if the Duke of Edinburgh did plan to have his daughter-in-law bumped off? What if ....? What if ....?

An American friend asked me "What if Kazim had been an Italian and not a Turk? Would you still have organized to have a hairdresser visit him. Would you have taken the mountain to go to Mohammed?"

Americans are persistent interrogators.

"With a name like Kazim he's hardly likely to be Italian but it's a very good question" I replied.

"He had no extended family to call the cops. Just an underground mafia into drug deals and pimping, who have the longest memories and revenge is their highest code of honour. What if I hadn't had that fast car? Would I have done what I did using either my Renault 4 or my Fiat 500, my 'chink'?" I tried, I really did, to analyse all that Astrid related stuff objectively but any synthesis just spat out a regurgitation of that timeless egg and chicken syndrome.

I could go on back to how I got to know Edward and how he gave me that fast car if you really want to go down the line of cause and effect.

A fairly reasonable starting point could be when I patched up my ex-wife's leaking second marriage. If you really work back down the line, my decision to make sure that that marriage worked, led to my being given the fast car that allowed me to be a getaway driver and more, or worse, depending how you look at it.

My daughter's mother had remarried an accountant. After the marriage appeared not to be working, I went over to London to look after my eight-year-old daughter while her mother went to the US on business. Her husband came to see me and asked how he could win back his new wife. I gave him the advice a friend had suggested: Get off her back, leave her alone and trust your luck.

A week later, my daughter's mum came back from the US as her father was seriously ill. I returned to Italy. Just before Christmas, her new husband called and said he'd taken my advice and it had worked. They'd met by chance on a bus and had got back together again. He thanked me.

For a couple of years there were no problems seeing my daughter. The second marriage seemed to be working.

Then the difficulties began. First Steppy asked me to have my daughter's name removed from my passport. No problem.

"We can do that in a couple of minutes." said the man in the passport office. "It's the other way round that can take ages."

Then I had to apply through lawyers to see my daughter "like normal people do".

An upcoming granted access was then withdrawn as "I gave it out of the kindness of my heart which was a mistake".

This went on and got worse. Much worse, especially after I gave up the job of looking after a neighbour's house in Italy that paid my daughter's mother a monthly maintenance cheque.

The only way Steps could adopt my daughter without my consent was to paint me out as a far too dangerous, drug and alcohol dependent good-for-nothing, to remain my daughter's legal father.

I struggled to prevent him adopting her. I fought for all I was worth which was a lot less than he was valued at. Rapidly running out of ammo, I weighed up whether to risk an almost certain suicidal bayonet charge or to raise a white flag when, like a tank attack and an airstrike rolled into one, the cavalry in the person of Edward showed up just in the nick of time.

Edward said he would take on my case as, he believed, though I was no saint, I was being unjustly treated. Over several weeks in his little library in Shangri-La, overlooking the olive trees that produced the best olive oil in the world, he prepared my case, assembling letters, drawings and information covering the twelve years of my relationship with my daughter. When he was done he sent the package with covering letters to a firm of prestigious solicitors in London who, he said, owed him some. It wouldn't cost me a lira. It took two years for things to work their way through the courts in London. Eventually I was interviewed by the Official Solicitor to the Appeal Court and six months later my ex-wife and her husband abandoned their case as a lost cause. We'd won on a technical knock out!

I now seriously owed Edward. Not money as there was never a question of that. How do you repay an unpayable debt?

Back when we'd finished a session of going through my daughter's letters and discussing strategy, Edward would gather the papers together in an orderly way and put them in a file. Then he'd pour us each a glass of whisky and we'd chat about things like the price of olive oil, the Asian front in World War II or the state of Italian rugby football. He called it rugger. At one of these after work chats, I asked him how his step son was doing. Edward's second wife had two sons, one of whom Edward put through Oxford university making sure he got all the best services and perks as the son of a dark blue alumnus. The other son seemed to do nothing much. This was the one I asked about.

It was as if I'd pulled a loose piece of wool from a badly knitted pullover: it began to unravel. Edward started to exude complaints about this stepson who thought of himself as an architect and had taken charge of the restoration work still under way on Shangri-La. When Edward was going through the accounts with him he discovered a large sum of money had gone missing and wanted an explanation. The stepson, all huffily, said he'd willingly drop the job if Edward wasn't happy with his work.

The stepson regularly invited his friends to parties by the swimming pool at Shangri-La and they'd leave empty glasses, bottles and full ashtrays for someone else to clear up. Edward bought a brand new family car for everyone to use and put it in the son's name, as he had Italian residency. After the stepson used it, the fuel tank was always just about empty.

Edward's grievances went on unravelling until the badly knitted pullover was just a tangle of spent wool lying in the middle of the study floor. It was if I'd unblocked years of built up resentment.

Then he started on his second wife. She demanded they dress for dinner. She insisted on being seen at the smartest horse race meetings. She was furious when he gave me a 5 litre flagon of their olive oil. And she smoked. In a matter of several minutes he'd pulled his second marriage apart and all that and those that went with it lay in shreds.

Within a few months his second wife and her son were out of Shangri-La. Edward divorced her but bought her a cottage in England and paid her a generous monthly allowance.

About this time Tigerlily came on the scene.

In the build up to Britain handing Hong Kong back to China, Edward made a pile of money winding up or restructuring British companies in the Far East. He employed three investment fund managers to handle his capital gains. Two were British men and they turned in annual average yields of around 15 to 20%. The third manager was Chinese and turned in annual averages of between 35 to 40%. The third fund manager was a woman - Tigerlily.

They became friends. One evening at some smart club function in Singapore, Edward was trying to avoid someone he didn't need to talk to but saw himself getting cornered. He noticed Tigerlily sitting alone so he asked her to dance. That was how they became friends, very good friends.

Tigerlily began to spend time in Italy and started to take an interest in the management of Shangri-La. This was at the same time as Edward's embittered, ex-second wife began legal proceedings to squeeze as much out of him as she possibly could. It began to seem that even Shangri-La might be threatened by her greed, egged on, no doubt, by her recently disinherited son.

Since my relationship with my daughter had resumed, thanks to Edward, I saw quite a lot of him and Tigerlily when they were in Italy. When they told me of their problems I said I knew a notary in Rome who could probably help. I said I'd call Donatella and afterwards call Edward in Singapore.

Donatella is the notary I went to when I agreed to buy the farm twenty something years earlier. The mediator who was arranging my buying the farm decided to go to her when we found a queue a mile long at the office of the other notary in Cortona. Donatella spoke English too. She handled all the legal work involved in the purchase and even waited for the taxes and fees until we were able to repay her. She remained close friends with my sister, brother and I for many years and followed the ups and downs of our fortunes. Donatella had reassured me after reading the long indictment from my daughter's stepfather's lawyers when he was trying to smear me as an undesirable character, unfit to be my daughter's father. Cheek! Donatella explained that re-phrasing my backing my car into a drainage ditch with my daughter on board as driving into a ravine was a normal legal tactic and she encouraged me to reply to all the accusations in detail.

As her role as vice-mayor of Cortona she'd encouraged my contributions to the cultural programmes of the town. Even when she moved back to her family practice in Rome she remained a special friend as well as a kind of guardian angel. At the end of one of our meetings about divorce settlements, water rights, laws about setting up educational associations or inheritance taxes, she offered me the keys to her house on one of the islands off the west coast of Sicily. I offered her the keys of my house in the mountains in exchange.

"No" she smiled brown eyed at me across the wooden expanse of her desk. "It doesn't work quite like that. I offer you my keys and you offer someone else your keys. They offer others their keys and somewhere, way way down the line, if it all works out, someone offers me their keys."

When I called her in her offices, we agreed on a date and time to meet. I called Edward in Singapore and he flew into Rome on the scheduled date. I met him at the airport and we drove to Donatella's grand studio offices in the heart of the city in a famous palazzo off the Corso.

Tigerlily was already there having flown in earlier from London. We sat at Donatella's large desk and Edward explained the problem. Donatella listened attentively. I occasionally helped in interpreting. When Edward had finished, Donatella reached out and picked up various objects on her desk; a pen case, a book, a packet of cigarettes, a lighter. She went through them one by one.

"Tell me if I've got this right. This is the house, this is the garden, this is the olive grove and this is the garage and the pool. Right?"

"Exactly" said Edward and Tigerlily simultaneously.

Donatella studied the objects a bit longer, then like the gully gully man in Port Said in Egypt or one of those three card hustlers who play small crowds on the street off a packing case, she rearranged them in front of her. When they fell into place to her satisfaction, she looked up smiling and said *"Ecco fatto."* Voila!

Tigerlily beamed Edward one of her classic full-frontal dental smiles. Donatella drafted a document, read it through as I interpreted, and that was it. We rose to go and she said the finished document would be ready in two weeks and she'd have it mailed to Edward in Singapore.

Tigerlily asked how much they owed her?

"Nothing" said Donatella smiling. "Friends of Martin's are friends of mine."

We thanked her and left. I thought I'd gone some way in repaying Edward for what he'd done for me.

When Astrid arrived back in Italy with her boyfriend Ron, they came to stay in my house.

They arrived on a Saturday. On the Sunday I was invited to lunch at the house of the family that looked after Edward's olive grove. I called and asked if I could bring two guests. No problem.

I drove Astrid and Ron to the house up the winding road near Shangri-La. With the whole extended family we had their normal Sunday lunch: *crostini* with bird liver pâté, pasta with bird kidney ragù, mixed roast bits of various birds, roast potatoes, salad and lots of the family's homemade wine. Afterwards it was cakes, coffee, *vinsanto* and the usual short business talk about the olive oil yield, a group photograph, then it was time to go.

As we said our goodbyes to the family, Tigerlily invited the three of us back to Shangri-La.

There, Edward showed Astrid and Ron around the large house and garden while I chatted to Tigerlily. When the others came back from their tour Tigerlily said they had something for me.

We all followed her outside to the garage.

Edward unlocked and opened the garage doors. There inside was a gun-metal, light blue-grey Volkswagen Mark II Golf turbo diesel car with Swiss registration plates.

Tigerlily handed me the keys.

I thought I still owed Edward some but was surprised how unflabbergasted I was. I thanked them anyway. This was the former stepson's car. *Merci bien. Moltissime grazie. Muchos graz.* etc.

As I had to drive my Renault 4 home I handed the keys of what was fast on its way to becoming the getaway car to Astrid. She could drive it home, or wherever.

3
The City of Gold

The modern German word for ore, as in iron ore, is *ertz*. The word is derived from the name of the capital of the easternmost province of Tuscany in central Italy where I first met Astrid and we laid the foundations of our later sins and the repercussions that followed in their wake. The town is called Arezzo.

During the centuries before the birth of Christ, the age of the Etruscans and later, the Romans, Arezzo was famous for its metal work; bronze (the alloy of tin, copper and, yes, arsenic in the early bronze age until the high death rate of metal workers made a switch to lead more practical) and iron. A Roman bride-to-be's gift list has come down to us and she includes specifically Etruscan cutlery from Arezzo; she wanted the best!

Gold is the metal that is the main driving force

of the local economy today. More gold jewellery is made in Arezzo than any other town on earth. There are over one thousand gold working establishments ranging from vast factories turning out gold chain by the kilometre down to small artisan workshops hand making designer jewellery and hardly a week goes by without a gold related robbery.

Arezzo is pronounced as if there was a 't' in it. Aretso! The 'Z' originated from the Etruscan alphabet. It came after their letter 'F' in alphabetical order but was dumped by the Romans and replaced by the 'G'. Only later, the Romans wanted it back but, as its place had been taken by the G, they stuck it on the end of the alphabet where it remains to this day.

During the dark decades leading up to the demise of the first millennium, when western Christian society sincerely believed they were doomed and the world was about to come to an end, the dreaded so-called Y1K milestone, church choirs were almost exclusively manned by males. Boys and men sung at the masses and services throughout the Christian calendar year and they learnt the repertoire by ear and heart. Boys being boys, as they approached their teens, their voices broke as their balls dropped. Those young men still singing who went on to become the tenors, baritones and basses of those dark ages had to learn a completely new repertoire. It took a decade to teach a chorister all the works to be sung, sometimes more than once a day, in the services of the church liturgical year.

A monk called Guido who lived in a monastery in Arezzo set out to solve the problem of learning music by ear and heart and replacing it with a system that relied on the eye and brain. Guido Monaco, as he is called today, drew four lines across sheets of vellum and noted the position and duration of notes in a scale of one to eight with squares and blobs that had different tails like varieties of cubistic tadpoles. He invented a system of musical annotation that allowed the choristers to read the notes as opposed to having to learn them. This meant a choir could master a repertoire inside a year instead of a decade.

As the year 1000 passed Armageddon-less, the western Christian world breathed a sigh of relief and got on with life and living. Guido's system, with a few modifications such as the introduction of a fifth line, is the basis of written music today. The town of Arezzo holds an annual international festival of choral works to celebrate Guido and his statue graces the roundabout in the circular square named after him, just up from the Arezzo railway station.

The railway station was built on the Campo di Marte, the field of Mars, a large open space just outside the city walls where soldiers once, long before, carried out military exercises. When the old medieval walls of Arezzo were torn down under the orders of Grand Duke Cosimo di Medici around 1560, to be replaced by modern fortifications defended by and from artillery, workmen dug up an Etruscan bronze life-size statue of a lion with a goat's head sticking out of its back. This was the mythical beast, the Chimera. It originally had the tail of a snake but that was never found. What they didn't find either was a life-sized statue of a winged horse named Pegasus carrying a rider called Bellerophon, a mythological Corinthian, who hunted down and killed the Chimera. The horse and rider were part of the sculptural composition and they're probably still somewhere buried under what is now the main municipal car park.

Arezzo is full of surprises. Tourists tend to go for one thing: the deservedly famous frescoes of the Legend of the True Cross by Piero della Francesco in the church of San Francesco. When they've seen those, they have a coffee, perhaps wander up to the Piazza Grande and have lunch, maybe catch the Cimabue crucifix in the church of San Domenico, then they leave with only the tip of the cultural and historical iceberg in their digital cameras and boxes.

Arezzo is where techniques of industrial mass-production were first used. In the dying years of the Roman Republic, a generation or so before the birth of Christ, Aretine potters employed craftsmen to carve scenes of Greek and Etruscan mythology in small shallow wooden reliefs. The potters impressed these reliefs into the soft inner surfaces of freshly thrown clay bowls, cups or plates, along with other decorative carvings. When these moulds dried they were centred on a potters' wheel and fresh clay was worked into them taking up the negative images. The moulds and contents were put aside to dry and shrink just enough so that after two or three days the moulds were upturned and the cups, bowls or plates were released with the impressions of the carved images embedded in relief in their outside surfaces. They were then fired into finished utensils. The moulds could be reused hundreds of times. No expensive hand painting was required. The brightness of the fired clay gave the pots the characteristic deep red-orange colour and with their lively, often erotic, imagery, *sigilata aretina*or Aretine coralware became extremely popular throughout Europe and the near east and put most of the costly hand-painted pottery trade out of business. At the peak of the industry, over one hundred factories turned out Aretine coralware by the thousands, each piece carrying the name of the factory owner, more often a freed slave, imprinted on it and they were exported all over the early Roman Empire. The Archaeological Museum in Arezzo, built into the ruins of a Roman amphitheatre, has a section devoted entirely to this remarkable industrial and artistic process.

Unfortunately for Arezzo, however, but setting an all too familiar precedent for the later industrial world, the simple ingenuity of the mass-production process contained the seeds of its own destruction.

Around 50 AD, a worker in one of the factories began surreptitiously removing samples from his workshop. Over the months he built up a collection of bowls, cups, jugs, plates and vases. One night he loaded a wagon with his samples and set off for Gaul, present day France.

If he had worked in the glass industry in Venice in the 16th or 17th centuries and had done to the Most Serene Republic what he did to the city of Arezzo, the Council of Ten would have ordered him to be hunted down to the ends of the earth by the Venetian secret police who, when they inevitably would have found him, would have gouged out his eyes with their daggers for running off with trade secrets like that.

But that Aretine potter was centuries ahead of the game and he got away with it. In Lyon, where the clay was almost identical to that in Arezzo, he set up a factory bypassing the expensive part of the Aretine process: carving the intricate wooden patterns to impress into the moulds. He had moulds made from the samples in his stolen collection. His factory turned out coralware almost as good as the originals at a fraction of the cost, flooding the markets right across the Roman Empire and by about 50AD, all the coralware factories in Arezzo had gone to the wall. A cautionary tale.

Shards of Lyon coralware still turn up in archaeological digs as far flung as Egypt and Scotland, North Africa and Austria. The most famous and comprehensive set of Lyon coralware to come down to us was delivered to an address in a town in southern Italy in the summer of 79AD and lay unpacked for nearly two thousand years. The town was Pompeii.

There's another local gem that rarely gets the publicity it deserves. We hear about the Piero della Francesco frescoes, Vasari the first art historian and Petrach the poets' houses, the piazza Grande and the Giostre alla Saraceno, the annual jousting event, but we rarely hear about an extremely famous bridge. It's not far from Arezzo.

If you take one of the roads to the Casentino and the Pratomagna areas, the mountainous forested regions north of Arezzo, there's a stone bridge that crosses the river Arno. It's called Ponte di Buriano. It is narrow and has five arches. This is the most photographed bridge in Italy, if not the whole world. It has been snapped a trillion times more than the Ponte Vecchio in Florence or the Bridge of Sighs in Venice, the Golden Gate bridge in San Francisco, London Bridge, the Fourth Bridge, the Fifth Bridge, the Bridge over the river Kwai (aka The Bridge over Troubled Waters), the bridges of Maddison county, the bridge over Antietam creek below Sharpsburg in Maryland, lots of bridges and let's leave it at that.

Yet all those amateur photographers don't even realise they're taking a picture of the Buriano bridge. They probably don't even see it like most of the visitors to this famous museum called the Louvre in Paris as they're too busy taking photographs to see what they're photographing. They photograph the bridge in their hundreds of thousands each day of each week, through armour plated glass and are surveilled by watchful guards and closed-circuit video cameras. The Ponte di Buriano features in the background, along with a spectacular range of mountains, in what is undoubtedly the most famous painting in the world: the Mona Lisa.

Close to the church of San Francesco is the Church of the Badia, and is spotted by its bizarre tower. The facade is a jigsaw puzzle of different building styles and remodellings, changes of mind and bishops. The interior is dark, appropriately, and many of the paintings that once hung on its walls have been stolen. But its prize is the cupola or the dome. You should walk down the central nave towards the altar and, keeping your head bowed, just watching your step, stop about five metres from the altar where you'll see a brass disc set into the floor. Here you halt and look up. There it is! The inside of a dome in all its intricate, architectural splendour with daylight filtering through the lantern at the summit. Once you've grasped the *trompe l'oeil* effect, keep your eyes focused upwards and take a couple of steps forward or sideways. Don't trip on the rope of the barrier which is there to stop you stealing any more of the church's depleted collection of pictures, but see how the cupola changes. It's a trick of illusion but it livens up the otherwise rather austere interior and being on the ceiling, it's virtually impossible to steal.

Another of Arezzo's many artistic jewels is the painted wooden crucifix by the 14th century artist Cimabue who taught Giotto, according to Vasari, the first art historian who had a house just around the corner. Cimabue's crucifix hangs above the altar in the church of San Domenico. Tourists and pilgrims walk down the stone paved road from the cathedral, past magnificent Renaissance buildings on either side, then at a fountain, they take a sharp right and go on to the piazza and church of San Domenico. If they went straight on at the fountain and down the steep hill, at the bottom on the right, they'd reach the Museum of Medieval and Modern Art. They seldom do, which is a pity as this museum has the largest collection of Madonnas of Mercy under one roof, not just in Italy, but in the whole world.

There are six of them in the museum. There are another two in the Lay Society building off the Piazza Grande and one in the church of Santa Maria delle

Grazie just on the edge of the town. There's even one by Giorgio Vasari himself in the Museum of the Works of the cathedral dating to 1553, a round painting or a *tondo*, painted on canvas. That makes ten Madonnas of Mercy in Arezzo alone. Venice comes second with five. Siena has four, Florence three, Pienza two and France has one. Germany has one too. The rest of the world, as far as I know, has none.

It's an icon showing the Virgin Mary standing centrally in the picture holding her cloak outstretched and sheltering a group of little people who stand or kneel under her protection. The icons vary in size and are made with different techniques. There's a silver gilt statue less than a foot high in the Mus of Med and Mod in Arezzo. Paintings of her are mainly on wood and range in size from almost miniature to the height of a person. Frescos, some of which have been removed from their original walls and remounted, are much larger. There are stone reliefs and painted wooden sculptures of the Lady. There are two coloured ceramic versions of her in Anghiari, site of a famous battle.

The Madonna of Mercy was the symbol of the Lay Societies, groups of middle class citizens who, during the late Middle Ages, administered charities, hospitals and justice, donated dowries for the daughters of their poorer members and said masses for their dead. They became increasingly powerful during the 15th and 16th centuries in towns like Arezzo until they were eventually suppressed by the Medici in Florence.

In Venice, the Madonna of Mercy was the protectress for the members of the Venetian Schools which performed an almost identical role as the Lay Societies, and were eventually suppressed by the ruthless Council of Ten.

The Madonna of Mercy also became a favourite protectress against the plague that regularly ravaged central Italy and the rest of Europe.

Back in the Mus of Med and Mod with all six of its Madonnas of Mercy, there's a large painting that hangs on the wall of the wide staircase between the ground and first floors. It's a panoramic landscape of the countryside just northeast of the city walls of Arezzo, showing several large villas, farmhouses and the hills that protect them from the north wind, and was the exclusive area where the richest people had their villas. One of these villas belonged to a family called *Occhini* or Little Eyes.

It was at a school in the villa in this painting that I first met Astrid.

4

The School

The school was set up in the late nineteen eighties by a group of Americans in their thirties and forties, and was based on a series of therapy schools in the US, particularly California, to educate and re-educate young people who weren't fitting into the American school system. It was also a way of providing a comfortable living in Bella Italia for an earlier generation of American misfits who thought they'd figured out how to fit in.

Mountains or deserts were favourite locations for therapy schools in the US. The founders of this school figured Italy and Italians would act as a deterrent; the language and culture substituting a desert or a mountain range. They would act as an invisible barrier and deter kids from making a run for it. That was one of their first mistakes.

The villa is a beautiful 16th century country

palazzo with some not-so-beautiful later additions. It is set in several hectares of land with vineyards and orchards. Two pillars straddle the gateway and broken terracotta lions top the pillars giving newcomers a sense of misgiving yet curiosity. Didn't anyone care about those terracotta lions, those first impressions?

Through the gate the road runs between an avenue of cypress trees leading up to the entrance, where a double marble stairway leads to the main door. Above the door is a large stone carved heraldic shield with the two pairs of eyes, the heraldic pun of the Occhini family.

The villa is conveniently close enough to Arezzo, yet lies in a country setting. It was ideal for the school in so many ways and the founders discovered they had an extensive reserve of local, English speaking, qualified and experienced teachers, therapists and administrators to draw on.

The problem with the villa was the monthly rent. It was astronomical. The Occhini family, their heirs or the trustees of their estate, probably couldn't believe their good fortune when these naive, idealistic Californians took over.

From the point of view of the school administration, all expenses were paid in Italian lire, whereas all income was in US dollars. This meant the school's economic success or failure was completely dependent on exchange rates between the two currencies.

The founders and their fellow colleagues purchased smart, expensive cars and generally set themselves up in fancy lifestyles. Exchange rate fluctuations were not top of their agendas. Another big mistake.

I don't want to come over all negative about the school. I'm sure a lot of the kids got much out of it. As a teacher I certainly did. There were many great educational and cultural projects, almost all initiated and executed by the local expat recruits. They saw the school as a way of working in a creative environment and a means to realise some of the ideas they wouldn't have been able to achieve otherwise, even though some of the American methods were unusual.

Many of the kids got a lot out of the school that they wouldn't have in any other educational establishment elsewhere because of the peculiar mixture of cultural backgrounds of everyone involved. It was at its best, a vibrant learning experience for teachers and students alike.

Then Saddam Hussein invaded Kuwait and the value of the US dollar began to slide in the wake of Desert Storm. As costs rose and income dropped, a gaping hole began to open up in the school's finances. I was only too aware of it, being a member of the executive committee which seemed to spend precious time discussing what was a fair free lunch for staff, one or two bread rolls, than addressing the bigger issues. When the headmaster pinched my butt going into one of our meetings, my suspicions became fears, wondering how long the school could last.

At the time the finances began to go down the tubes a new generation of kids came in, much smarter and more street wise than their predecessors. They quickly discovered that out there in Italy you were quite safe to travel and Italians would feed and look after you. The invisible barbed wire fence of the Italian language and culture became shown up for what it was. It wasn't. The whole of the earlier system of rules and conventions within the school began to unravel. Much of the new recruitment was by word of mouth from kids returning to the States. As the discipline crumbled, so the word of mouth recruiting system dried up.

I was convinced the writing was on the wall when a tree was ceremoniously planted to commemorate the death of an early benefactor of the school. A few months afterwards the tree died of neglect.

But then it was at the School that I met Astrid and things were never to be the same again.

One morning there she was at the bottom of a flight of steps leading out of the school building with four other students standing around talking to her. A thump of recognition punched my solar plexus, something that happened only when I met someone who I knew I was going to meet from some way back premonition. It had happened rarely before but enough to recognize the feeling as you know the first tremors of an imminent earthquake. She was tallish, gangly almost with her long skinny legs and thin in a school where the girls tended to add being overweight to their other problems. She had short, reddish-blonde, wavy hair and her mouth was small and delicate, a thin nose and sparkling brown, almond shaped eyes. I knew from the word go that she was special, set apart from the rest, and she had the air of knowing it too.

On her arrival, the teachers had been briefed as we always were on the arrival and background histories of new inmates at regular staff meetings.

Astrid was fifteen. She'd already lived more than anyone twice her age. Bright and intelligent, with good grades in all subjects except math, she was just recovering from having been kidnapped by the father of her best school friend. After a state-wide search across California, the couple had been arrested. Her father, a lawyer who'd helped the school out of some of its early legal quagmires, sent her to Italy; effectively, like so many of the pupils' parents, passing the buck.

There were no black and white guidelines circumscribing staff-student relationships whether in the academic or the therapy areas. It was left as a tacit understanding that common sense would prevail. So it was a bombshell exploding amongst the somnambulistic community when one of the female students, before entering one of the most stringent ordeals in their steady progression towards graduation, confessed that a man on the therapy staff had kissed and fondled her, with her consent, on several of the recent school excursions. This girl was one of my best students. The staff member was one of my best friends. He and his wife were frequent visitors to my farm and she was pregnant with twins. I was in line to be godfather to one of them. As a friend and as a member of the executive committee, I acted as a go-between and tried to get to the truth, the bottom line of what had been going on. My friend denied any messing around with the girl but, his wife being in the advanced stages of pregnancy, I knew how frustratingly randy a father-to-be could get. Also the girl was extremely attractive. In the end, the couple were suspended. Their babies were born and they left Italy shortly afterwards. Back in the USA the twins went on to become highly successful soap opera stars.

Even in the aftermath of what happened, or didn't, no guide lines were set up. Staff were continually being faced with sexually challenging situations. An English teacher arriving at the school for the first time was confronted by the sight of a male therapist lying on his back in the middle of the floor of the entrance hall with three female students lying face down on top of each other on top of him. Even though the teacher was British, the scene sent out quite a clear signal. In this school, they do things differently.

I taught a variety of subjects; art and art history to begin with. The school needed a teacher of American history so I said I'd give it a whirl. Keeping one week ahead of my class I scraped by until we hit the Civil War and watched, week after week, the award winning TV series on videos. I became hooked on Hooker, Lee and Grant et al. It took me years to shake off that addiction. I even tried Civil War rehab which helped but I still have occasional relapses just as I love the smell of a good cigar.

Another class I taught was photography. It was still a time, not so long ago, before digital cameras. Most of the kids had (analogue) cameras and we'd go out on shooting expeditions. I converted a bathroom in the villa into a darkroom and lent my enlarger, developing and fixing dishes to the enterprise. I mentally made a rule that I would never work in the darkroom with less than two students at one time. When you're bending over a swishing, developing image in the intimate darkness with a red light glowing, or bumping into each other as you reload a film can in complete darkness, touching each other surprisingly in protruding spots, it's innocent enough, exciting even, if it never goes beyond that. I think the kids liked it for that as much as the photography so I had my rule. Never less than two students in the darkroom with me was my rule so that it would never end up as her word against mine.

One afternoon, a girl who was passionate about photography, arrived at the darkroom at the appointed time. We waited for her co-sign-inner who didn't show up. We waited and waited but still she didn't arrive. I told the girl I was sorry but had to cancel the class and she was distraught. She was one of my best students too. When I gave her and her group the last of their external assignments, going off all morning with one shot in the camera - I'd fired off 23 of their 24 shots before they left - some of them came back in tears, others angry. She'd come back with a triumphant grin having bagged a car smash on a zebra crossing in town. She pleaded with me but I stuck to my rule. When she started to cry I finally gave in and we spent two hours in that dark room under the red light. She was a victim of severe abuse as a child in Eastern Europe, had been adopted by an American family and abused by her adopted father too, along with her sister, before they were both sent to the school in Arezzo. Close quarters bumping into each other, chatting, getting excited as a new image emerged beneath the slap lapping developer, knowing what she'd been through and what was going through her mind as her tit hit my elbow for the thirteenth time, gave me the shivers. When we finally emerged into the afternoon light streaming through the villa window, I breathed a sigh of relief. I hoped I still had my job.

With Astrid all caution flew right back out of the window. It was like all the rules just didn't apply any more, the unwritten rules too.

She shone in all my classes. In art history, the practical side, she was the best gold water gilder I have ever seen, applying gold leaf certainly as well if not better than any of the assistants of Duccio or Giotto. In cartography she was elegantly precise. She enjoyed her work and was highly dedicated. But she wanted something more: At some point we got talking about music and playing musical instruments and I said I played the penny whistles. I'd played the trumpet since the age of twelve, saxophone, clarinet later, passing through piano and guitar stages. Penny whistles were the way I hung on to playing musical instruments without having to practise hours every day or being lumbered with carrying a heavy instrument like a double bass case from one gig to the next.

Astrid said she wanted to learn to play the penny whistle. She said she wanted lessons. I checked with the head of the academic staff and the idea was OK'd. Lessons were to take place after lunch in my classroom.

This should never have been allowed to happen.

My classroom was set apart from all the others. It had a separate entrance from the front terrace. For several weeks, this pretty sixteen year old gangly girl with her fluffy, rusting, blonde hair, her almond eyes and infectious laugh would knock on the door, enter and sit down in my classroom, just the two of us. I taught her how to hold the whistles keeping a thumb and little finger in control always; how to breathe and time her breathing with pauses in the music. I never learnt circular breathing but got her to work on her diaphragm and to ingest nasally as she exhaled orally. She was a natural. She was excellent. Then it got intimate. I'd sit behind her and place my arms around her and my hands over hers, my finger tips resting on hers as she held the whistle in her mouth. I told her to raise her fingers if she felt my fingers rise above hers. It was a way for her to learn fingering. It was also a way for us to get close together without actually getting it on. We even swapped spit as we exchanged whistles.

I don't remember what put a stop to those classes, but I came away at the end thinking that at least I still had my job - almost.

We played two tunes at the school's Thanksgiving concert in her last year: Greensleeves and an Irish jig from a Chieftains album I'd learnt. We got a round of apples and pears and she gave me a big hug. Then, one day outside a stone cottage, on a hill below Cortona, where a group of students was spending the day with one of the local staff, Astrid and I said goodbye and gave each other a farewell hug, half hoping, at least I was, that wasn't going to be the end of things between us.

A year or more after she left Italy, the school finally gave up the struggle against plunging recruitment, an ever-weaker dollar and the gaping black hole of debt. From one day to the next we went from being salaried academics to salad dressing. I packed up my classroom, drove home to my hillside retreat, pulled out a typewriter and began to write.

5

Lighting fires

Astrid called me on Thanksgiving one year after our penny whistle concert. She was staying with another former alumnus in South Carolina and told me she was planning to come to Italy next year and we must get together. I described the terracotta heads stashed away in a box along with all the other shards, broken pipes, bits of bicycles and dangerous insects in the darkness beneath the steps of the villa in Arezzo. I'd rescued two of the smallest and put them in the history classroom, the sunniest, happiest classroom in the school where I'd taught Astrid to make maps, frescoes, apply gold-leaf and egg-tempera to wood panels and to play the penny whistles. Months later, she wrote and told me about herself. Did I get her card from Gettysburg? (She knew I was a Civil War ex-addict struggling in rehab but had managed to stop using.) She was going steady, dating as she described it, which I took to mean anything from holding hands in the cinema to rutting like bucks and does. The English call it seeing someone. He was called Ron and Astrid said she really got on with his mom.

She'd enrolled in an Italian language course at the University for Foreigners in Perugia the following summer and "we are going to get together and drink and smoke, and do all the things we weren't allowed to do at school."

I began to imagine all the things we might do that we weren't allowed to do at school without the written rules inhibiting us.

Another postcard from her the next spring said she was different, grown up, her hair was long and we were going to hang out together. Hang out? Did that mean we were going to see each other often? Once, back in school, she'd shown me a sore she had in the back of her mouth. She opened wide and I peered into the wet, pink depths and saw right down inside her. That sort of seeing?

Little Belle from Virginia came to stay for the summer, to paint her heart out downstairs in what had once been one of the stables in my house. She'd been a student on a studies abroad programme in Tuscany with a posh New York art school. The association I worked with had organised it all. She had written and asked if she could stay in my house.

She arrived, short and chubby, with plenty of warning. Her turpentine supply had spilt in her suitcase so she smelt oily as we sat out on the loggia in the after-dinner dark.

Some women have these great opening lines as if to set the parameters, just to get things warmed up. "My father killed himself" one woman said to me right at the start of our relationship which was just what I wanted to hear to get the juices flowing. It's like saying don't dump me as I've already survived the ultimate being dumped experience. Another erection wilting one-liner while we were actually going at it like rabbits was "I was raped in the arse so don't even think about going there." Woah! Whether I was or wasn't was behind the main point but it brought things quickly off the boil. This was original: "My brother held me down and his three friends raped me then he took his turn. I was only eleven." That is a really arousing start to foreplay. Rape is evil and damaging but there's a place to discuss the sexual body count and it's not before you're about to get into bed with someone.

Little Belle's tear-jerking appeal for the sympathy vote was "When I was a lot younger, my beloved brother went off into the woods and shot himself."

What are you meant to say? (a) I'm sorry. (b) I'm sad, or (c) Suggest we have another drink. The first toast that summer was to Little Belle's late brother.

One morning I asked her to iron some of my shirts as I fear and loathe ironing. Half way through the second shirt she broke down in tears saying ironing reminded her of her black nanny she'd had when she was a child. Her father, a US Senator, left her in her nanny's charge as he was too busy a body to bother and nanny had been more than a mom to her. Ironing brought it all back, along with the ghosts that abounded in her Charleston childhood garden of midnight evil spirits.

In the mornings Little Belle went jogging with her walkman though she didn't run, she hopped round the mountain road, or that's what it seemed like. She may even have lost a few ounces here and there, especially there.

I warned Little Belle that we were likely to have a visitor soon, an ex-student of mine with whom I had a 'special thing'. She didn't seem bothered and just continued painting her paintings of fountains and breaking things around the house in her accident-prone way.

With the date of Astrid's arrival approaching, I began to wonder what kind of conflagration lay waiting to happen just around the corner of that summer.

You light a fire and you put it out. When I was a kid at boarding school in Nairobi, Kenya, one Sunday when most of the inmates were away, out on leave, two of my mates and I went off into the forest among the extensive school grounds. We had a box of matches. We reached an area close to the boundary fence where the forest gave way to grassland bordering onto the Kikuyu tribal reserve. We lit a fire and beat it out. We lit another and before the wind got up, we smothered that too. Then we lit a third and the wind came in and fanned the flames and in seconds we knew this one had taken off. We fled, running through the forest back to the school buildings and, as we passed the deputy headmaster's house, I stopped and rang his doorbell. As he answered it, I said there was a fire in the forest and he sent out an alarm call. All the boys and masters not on leave-out or AWOL came to the rescue and after a couple of hours of sweat and smoke we extinguished the blaze.

There's nothing like the sparkling sizzle you get working alongside people who are swearing what they would do to the perpetrators of this crime while you're there helping them and you're responsible for that crime. There's a perverse kick in the gut you get hearing the deputy headmaster theorise as to the fire's origin in the Kikuyu reserve knowing he was about 400 metres off track.

There was nothing more zinglyish like the tingle that ran down my spine and back up the other side when I heard, next morning in school assembly, the headmaster thanking all those who'd helped extinguish the fire, and, in particular, the three boys who'd given the early alarm.

Astrid returned, as I knew she would. She arrived back with her boyfriend Ron at the beginning of July. I met them at a bar in town and gave her a huge hug. She looked great with her long, frazzled, jaggedy blonde hair, her slim athletic, sunburnt limbs scantily, summery khaki-clad, juggling with her contagious laughs. As I loaded their bags into my car she said to Ron:

"Don't mind us. Martin and I, we have a thing."

To this I silently agreed thinking "Yes, *and* I have a box of matches."

6

Unwritten rules

This is the distance my trust in her goes. I just get given a fast car with a sunroof and a top-of-the-market stereo system, a turbo-charged diesel engine that'll put me up with the serious contenders in the *autostrada* Golf stream circuit where you accelerate rather than brake to get out of trouble and I'm letting Astrid have firsties.

"Sure. Which is the indicator control?" she says without batting a wink.

My girl! Well not quite. First Ron has to leave which he obligingly does, forever. They get a train out Monday morning and I notice he buys a one-way ticket, whereas Astrid gets a return and she's back laughing the next weekend.

With Little Belle insisting she rides shotgun, she, Astrid and I test drive the car with Bolero loud on the sound system. We travel very very fast to the other side of Lake Trasimeno where Little Belle and Astrid go topless kayaking. Little Belle shows off her skills, twisting and turning and rolling over under water then showers off any lake water before we leave. Astrid says she'll wait and shower later, giving me a pre-meditated look and a laugh. On the way back we're pulled up by the traffic police and the car gets the first of many checkovers. The officers are curious about the ownership but we're cleared and allowed to go on home where, as the temperature is rising, at her request, I hose Astrid down out on the lawn, the first of our several aquatic sessions.

It's not easy for Little Belle and it's getting harder as the nights go by. When Astrid returns the following weekend and doesn't wake up in the bed she slept in the weekend before, Little Belle admits magnanimously:

"Well you got yourself a fast new car and the prettiest girl around. Looks like you hit the jackpot!"

Long after Little Belle has gone to bed Astrid and I sit up on the loggia and she feeds me pieces of her teenage life.

"I used to be an equestrian acrobat when I was younger you know, leaping off and jumping back on galloping horses and standing up in the saddle and stuff. Then I quit. It was really dangerous. I think I was trying to impress my mom. Did you know I was once a ballerina? I was even asked if I would join the state ballet company but I decided against it. Too much like a career. I got to be a table layer and, would you believe it, a flower arranger. I even won first prize. I won prizes at athletics too. I was school champion hurdler and we even travelled abroad to compete. On one of those trips, out at night, I went into this bar and played a slot machine and won the jackpot!"

I think she's trying to impress me. She pours us some more wine, re-arranges her skirts and lights a cigarette.

"I was a champion half-miler in my prime. I even beat the Kenyans." I'm trying to keep up, not to let the side down.

The next day she continues her inverted interrogation.

"One of my counsellors at school said I was ruthless."

As Astrid says this I'm preparing her favourite pasta: chopped tomatoes, basil, garlic with parmesan cheese and olive oil whizzed in the mixer and poured cold and raw over the hot spaghetti. Little Belle has tactfully gone off to Prague with a friend so we have the world to ourselves.

"My favourite! Yum! Do you think I'm ruthless?"

If in doubt, talk about food.

"How hungry are you?"

"Medium. Do you know Martin, when I finally made it to be a dorm head at school, and it was hard work getting that far, at night, after I'd made sure everything was locked up and everyone was in bed and asleep or pretending to be, I'd get into my bed and lie there and try and imagine what it would be like with you in bed with me."

"Game of dominoes?" I ask, totally at sea.

I'm not a novice in this area by any means but this girl is running rings around me. I used to be her teacher but who's running classes now?

A few days ago we went to a wedding. Astrid wore her long, tight red dress so you could see the indent of her navel in the tightly stretched fabric. I picked some bright red geraniums to match and pinned them in her tied back hair.

The wedding was at a stone farmhouse on top of a hill over-looking the upper river Tiber valley with the Mountains of the Moon beyond. One of the guests, Astrid's former councellor at school, asked Little Belle what was going on between Astrid and I but Little Belle blocked her. I avoided any one-to-one with former faculty as I didn't care what they thought. No one was going to wake me from this little number. The bride and groom led the family and guests up to the top of the hill behind the house and everyone stood holding hands in two concentric circles, as excerpts from The Prophet were read in three languages and an anvil-shaped cloud mushroomed in the pink glow of the sunset.

Pretty little girl with a red dress on lay asleep in the back of the car as Little Belle and I drove back late from the wedding. I played Glen Gould's versions of Bach's Goldberg Variations all the way to stifle any questions from the passenger riding shotgun.

Back home I carried Astrid from the car into the house and laid her on the sofa in the living room. Little Belle tactfully said goodnight. Not wanting Astrid to spoil her dress, I removed it and discovered, to her waking laughter, why she found the joke about underwear earlier that evening so funny. She wasn't wearing any!

Each night we tore out another page of the rule

book of acceptable behaviour and we drank vignettes of each other whose tastes, temperatures, textures, smells and sensations remain indelibly imprinted unprintably on that summer.

Before she went to sleep, she crawled around the bed and pillows on all fours, squashing out a little nest, just like a dog getting its basket ready. She said she was an animal, feral, and I believe she was.

Seven days later I'm floating gently down a warm river and she's in my arms, laughing. Way up above us trucks and cars rumble distantly across a concrete viaduct. We've just doused ourselves under a boiling hot sulphurous thermal jet of water and to cool off we drift under an old stone bridge and I snap one of the straps of her bikini top like a guitar string and she swims off to catch drips of water from underneath the arch of the bridge in her mouth. Wading, mud covered couples give us sideways glances as we climb back into the boiling mud pool and wash off more of our sins.

An hour before we committed a robbery. It was her idea but I was the accessory before and after the crime. She was the burglar and I was her getaway driver. I'd driven her to the old villa where the school had been and she'd walked up the cypress tree-lined drive carrying her rucksack, gone round and below the main entrance staircase and into the dark store where she'd loaded her rucksack up with three terracotta heads. We knew they were there as I'd taken two when I had a classroom right next door and kept them there on display. They were the broken off heads of statues that once stood on the roof of the villa back around 1570 and were lying discarded in a heap. We were rescuing them from their dark abandonment and showing them some tender loving care and appreciation. That's what we told ourselves and I'm sticking to it.

On a Sunday she's sitting on the *loggia* wearing her bikini and her face has black smudges. She's been busy every spare moment, cleaning one of her terracotta heads, part of her loot. She takes care over removing the paint from each curl of hair, gouging carefully with the little bradawl, removing the centuries of encrusted lime and dirt.

"How much do you think it's worth?" she asks, as if I know.

She puts the head down carefully, brushes off the white chips from her tummy and goes down into the garden and showers under the irrigation sprinkler. When she's thoroughly soaked, she comes up to me on the *loggia* and thrusts her head forward to give me a kiss and as I lean towards her receptively, she sprays me with water from her mouth, laughs and gives me a wet hug leaving damp patches on my clothes.

That night, lying in the night heat as the light Indian curtain wafts gently in the summer breeze, she takes my hand in hers and leads it on a guided tour. We are going to visit her special, favourite places, her secret, private spots.

Our first stop is a rib under her left arm. She doesn't say why it's special but I take her word for it and admire the atmosphere. It feels special, as if she'd pointed out a statue of historical and artistic importance. Then we're off again, up, over her tummy, past the well known landmark of her navel which isn't on the itinerary but nevertheless gets a mention by the guide as if, on our way from the Forum to the church of San Clemente in Rome, we pass the Colosseum. It's too prominent and famous a landmark not to point out. We're really heading for the tattoo, the quartered moon with its interwoven vine. The guidebook describes how she sought throughout the empire for an artist of special sensitivity and skill, who she could trust to draw it, working from her *sinopia,* or preparatory sketch, painfully in pricks of pinks and greens, as far below the Colosseum as any embarrassment and prudery allowed.

My fingers are a slow group. We want to take everything in. We don't want to miss any part of this tour. We suck in and swallow every detail. The five of us lap it all up. We want our money's worth as we've been saving for ages and ages for this trip of a lifetime. The guide waits patiently for us to catch up.

Reunited, we pause for a rest and trade *saliva gassata* for refreshment. Revived, her hand guides mine on, down a pathway that ends in a well tended garden laid out on a gentle rise. Like fearless children of not abusive but neglectful parents, our intertwined hands slip over the edge, she guiding the way, and we enter into her hidden cave behind the waterfall, her grotta, her most secret and private place. Few visitors are allowed here she tells the privileged tourists, only the very few specially invited guests. This, she confides, is where she comes sometimes when she's alone. Dark, damp and warm; very San Clementy.

Out from in between the sheets, when we

eventually come up for breathers as the going was getting hot and stuffy down under, in the dry night air I take her hand. I'm the guide now. I turn her over onto her itinerary and take her left hand and lead it willingly down to the base of her spine, to the little niche in its lowest bone. This is a spot I discovered exploring her gangly geology a few nights ago and I point it out to her, leading one of her fingers into its concavity. It's a rare, possibly unique example, of an indented coccyx I whisper into her ear and it should be a World Heritage Site. She gives a muffled laugh into the pillow when she realises what a treasure she's been sitting on for the last eighteen years, ten months and twenty three and three quarter nights.

One thing was certain: Astrid wasn't doing all this to get better grades in American history, art history, musical appreciation, botany or cartography, but she nevertheless got straight A plusses in what she did. Her homework was outstanding.

When I took Astrid to a concert in Cortona, a special French lady I knew whispered in my ear as we kissed the air beside each others' cheeks "Congratulations. She's lurvly. 'Ow deed you feind air?" Trust the French. A local count who caught us sitting together at a table in a corner in Bar Sport winked and said as he left, "Bravo." And trust the Italians.

Tigerlily was shocked yet she was half Edward's age. The rest of them pretended what was going on wasn't.

I knew we were asking for trouble so I kept what

I called my emotional crash helmet on and my sentimental seat belt firmly buckled up tight.

Little Belle gave up the struggle to keep her shotgun seat. She came back from Prague to find her worst fears confirmed. When I asked her if she'd sent me a postcard she said she'd thought about it and hadn't so I knew where I stood. When she finally went leaving Astrid and me to it, she left a trail of limited damage behind her. She broke a mirror cleaning up the bedroom and I wondered who was going to pay for the seven years bad luck. She went to meet her beau and if she'd picked up half the energy we'd given out she was going to eat him alive.

Astrid began to pack her bags too, though typically, she went about it in a round-about way. Not suddenly, but over a few days she began doing things differently. When she came home she started by talking about her new friends. Some were musicians. She wanted to spend more time with them. Then a new name crept into her vocabulary: Kazim. She met him through Mojo, an English drop-out in Perugia. Kazim scored dope for her quickly with no fuss or bother or beating about the bush.

Problems arose about her staying on in Italy. She said she wanted to live here but had to go back as her ticket and visa expired and her dad wasn't able or prepared to change things. She changed her mind about her last days. First she was coming to my house and we planned to go to the ocean, the Tyrrhenian Sea and the Island of Giglio. When I went to collect her in Perugia she was different, quiet. We sat across from the Etruscan gate and its arch framed her face.

Things weren't the same, could never be as they were before, she told me. She wasn't coming home either. Fine. I accepted everything. She wasn't sure where she was going but thought she'd probably follow the band. She was a groupie at heart, she smiled. I gave her the press cutting of the news of the death of her beloved Jerry Garcia. She'd described her Dead Head nights and how she'd followed that band and what they had meant to her. We'd played their tapes out driving and she'd gone into trances of improvised ecstasy. Handing her the obituary I could just as well have told her that one of her fathers had died. There were tears in her eyes and now, even more, she was determined to stay in Italy. She felt European, not American and because her favourite American was dead, she had no one left to go back to.

I took her to lunch at a little trattoria and she nibbled unhungrily and talked about her new friends and the music they played, and how they wanted her to sing with them. A young boy from another table in the restaurant came and stood behind her, fascinated, drawn to her. When I told her, she turned round and said *ciao*. The boy blushed. She might go for older men, she laughed but never the other way.

She walked with me towards the car and we left each other at the corner of the church in the piazza so neither of us could look back.

I hate August bank holiday. The heat, the crowds, the traffic. Across the valley, the smog above the *autostrada* turns from brown to orange at the beginning and end of this long weekend and there was a Monday in the middle just to prolong things. I planned to stay at home, whereas we'd planned to go to the sea.

I'd plant the Judas tree. I'd bought it for Astrid for its month of spring flowers, not for its name.

Halfway through the holiday, she phoned, out of the blue. She wanted to come over after all. Would I collect her from the train station that evening?

She was back to her laughing self, even when I told her we were staying home to clean the kitchen shelves and paint the dining and living rooms. She set about the jobs as if she was laying gold leaf. When we'd finished, I took her to the count's villa, the same count that had said bravo. The villa had a swastika and an eagle emblazoned on its front, from when it was the German headquarters fifty years earlier and she insisted on having her photo taken in front of it as a friend of hers back in the States was into that stuff. She hugged the tree that was over a thousand years old. We swam in the most beautiful pool in the world then she fell asleep in a deckchair.

She wanted to go back that evening, saying she'd call in a couple of days and come and spend her last weekend in Italy with me.

She didn't call for four days. Suddenly her voice was on the line asking if I would come and collect her in Perugia and we were going to have fun.

I could see the moment I met her in the piazza near her apartment that this wasn't going to be fun. She burst into tears and told me she didn't want to hurt me and I said I wouldn't let her. I'd worn my emotional crash helmet from the start. She wasn't going to spend the last two days with me. She wanted to follow the band. Could she come back to collect her things and say goodbye to the house and gardens? She'd been so happy there. It was her first real home.

She slept almost all the way back in the car, then back home she had a shower and I cooked mussels for dinner. She asked me for some more money and I wondered what had happened to the cheques she'd had two weeks ago and the other money I'd given her. When she'd packed her bag, stowing her terracotta head carefully in amongst her silk knickers, she walked around the gardens, the house and took a last look at the living room with farewell eyes, then it was down to the station. As her train pulled in I kissed the tears from her face, hugged her and she went off into the night.

7
The Plan

Big Pete gets up from the table in the tiny kitchen. He makes it seem even smaller every time he walks in the door. He collects the dirty dishes from our lunch and puts them into the sink. He doesn't even move his feet, just reaches across and drops them in. He'll wash them later, without rinsing them, the English way.

Big Pete is sizeably substantial. He'll find the weaker points in your furniture. Legs of chairs snap as he sits down for a game of dominoes or a table top can just as easily come away from the base frame as he leans against it, contemplating a backgammon move. He's gone through the old tiled floor of my kitchen twice, and on my birthday he lifted me up over his head and carried me through the streets of Cortona on our way to the pizzeria, and I'm not exactly a lightweight. He teaches martial arts and has a blaze of tattoos across his back and upper arms, and he's done time before both inside Her Majesty's youth hostel and in the army. Now he goes into his bedroom in this small, damp apartment to get changed and put on his working clothes.

Maria tells Astrid to sit down and keep still as she needs her hair doing. Astrid's going to have her hair tied back tight to her head where it can't get in her way or be used as a weapon against her as it has been recently.

The two of them couldn't be more different.

Astrid is tall (almost my height, but not as tall as Pete), slim as an Ethiopian marathon runner, slimmer than she was during the summer after the street life she's been living the last three months. She was always quite skinny, a race apart from most of her peers at school. Her hair, which Maria has started brushing, parting and weaving into braids, has grown much longer in the last two years; down to her shoulders, fair and wavy. It used to be a ruddy chestnut colour but she tinted it blonde when she graduated, thinking she'd have more fun and she was right. She wants to grow it down to her waist for when she's a famous singer. I've never heard her sing but have complete faith in her self-confidence.

Maria isn't tall. She's stocky with dark, smouldering eyes, rosy cheeks and short, jet black hair. She's a tough lady. She doesn't stand any messing about and makes good gravy. For Maria and Pete lunch is dinner and dinner is tea. I can never get used to drinking wine at tea but with them I do. She's wearing dark grey all over. So am I. It's better for working at night we believe, though none of us, except Big Pete, has ever done anything like what we're about to do. Astrid is wearing the red, polo-neck pullover (turtle-neck she calls it), my favourite. Her favourite now. She's tucked it into her jeans which makes her look even younger, more vulnerable. She's laughing as Maria pulls back her head again, clearing the decks.

Big Pete comes back into the kitchen, shrinking it again. He's wearing black, loose jogging trousers (pants, Astrid would call them), and a black T-shirt with a golden Chinese dragon splashed down the front like he spilt it. He's got dirty trainers on his feet. "Good grips" he grins. (I must get Astrid some decent boots soon.) His tattoos on his arms take on new, apotropaic dimensions, not that he needs that. Just to meet the size of those arms, that weight of muscle would scare the shit out of anyone who wasn't on his side. His small eyes are fiery, twinkling from inside his deep-set brows, under his close cropped hair which Maria mows regularly. He puts a knife onto the table in front of Astrid. It's a Stanley knife, a cutter. Astrid can't turn as her head's in Maria's grip but her eyes look down at the blade then up to him and she smiles.

Today, this evening, after dark, we're all going to give someone a haircut he'll remember for the rest of his life.

I'm the driver for this job. The get-there and get-away person. It wasn't Astrid's idea. She said I should stay out of this, but I said you need a good reliable driver on a job like this. You can't be worrying about directions, parking, keeping the engine running, concentrating on a smooth take-off afterwards when you've got so much else to think about and when it's done, you're going to be all wound up, emotional, except Big Pete. So I'm the driver. Besides, I've been Astrid's driver on a previous job back in the summer and I know she knows I'm reliable.

We'd finished lunch an hour ago when Astrid realises she's left her passport at home, so while I drive from the concrete sprawl into the hills above the ancient town to collect it, she goes through the details of the plan with Big Pete and Maria. I nearly collide with a heating fuel tanker coming towards me in the rain on my side of the road. That would really have screwed things up. When I get back to their apartment, Astrid has been through everything with them, all the possibilities, shown them the maps and the diagrams she'd drawn the night before, after she'd finished crying.

We're aiming for a little, two storied house, right off one of the main circular roads that runs just below and around the medieval walls of the city of Perugia she'll have explained. It's called 'the Mad House' as it was once the check-in and check-out place to the local asylum. Astrid's map shows how we get to it: keep going straight as we come out of the tunnel that cuts beneath the city, down fifty metres then sharp left and the little house is immediately at the corner on the right. There's a car park behind that we can use if there's space, but it's usually pretty crowded. There they'll leave me in the car with the engine running, walk to the house on the side away from the main road. Pete and Maria will wait in the dark behind the house while Astrid goes round to the entrance. She'll try the door with her key. If she can open it, he's out and they'll go in and collect her things, Astrid will leave her messages and we'll go. But that scenario will only get half the job done. Unsatisfactory she feels.

We've been through all the permutations. That's one. Another: she can't unlock the door as his key is in the lock inside so he's in there with the two dogs, Strega and Jazz. The dogs are smart she says, large and dangerous. She'll knock at the door. What is the man inside most likely to do? He's not expecting a visit. Probably come out onto the little balcony above the entrance, look below to see who's there, see her and come down and let her in. What then? Depends who's in there with him. If it's just the dogs, get them outside the house first. Who else could be there with him? His friends. Some dealers, stealers, users. How many of them could you expect at most? Four or five. Could Pete handle that many? What shape are they in? She describes them, the ones she knows. There's old Mario but he's an alcoholic, a real wino. Big Pete could flick him into a corner. The others? They could be Turks, Moroccans. They'd be scared though. More of Pete than him. He has some hold over them. They owe him somehow, but they'd probably make a run for it. They don't need more trouble, they've got enough as it is. Astrid is clear about this.

OK. So Astrid goes in and Maria comes up right behind her. Her job is to keep Astrid on the job. There's going to be some shouting and she mustn't be distracted. She knows where everything is, the stereo, the big knife. So: dogs out. Pete comes in. Visitors out.

Then what? Pete takes care of the guy while Astrid and Maria go up the spiral staircase, go through the bedroom, the pile of clothes in the corner, into the other room for the books, then back downstairs, get the stereo, leave her messages, then out into the car. Seconds later, Pete will follow, leaving someone with a short back and sides and a memento, a souvenir of the visit.

These are the plans. We're mad, crazy. Crazy about Astrid. We believe in her. Totally, as she would say.

Oh, she remembers, the place stinks. There could be dogshit too. It depends what time of the day it is, what state he's in, whether he's just shot up. Don't be put off by the smell she says. The taxi driver nearly vomited last week when she went back with Rosemary to collect some of her things.

You really wouldn't believe that Astrid is the brains behind this to look at her. She's an eighteen year old American girl who's had some family problems back home in California and spent a couple of years at the school in Arezzo where they tried to straighten her out, and apparently succeeded and she's recently completed a year in college in Maryland. How did she persuade us to go along with her I ask myself? Maria's just finished fixing her hair and I take a couple of photos of them both. You'd think they were going out to a party, or shopping, laughing like that. When the going gets tough, the tough get off their arses. Astrid's even wearing lipstick, something I haven't seen since the wedding in the summer, to match the red dress she wore. They've built a close bond between them, she, Maria and Big Pete over the last three days. We all have. United behind her, in front of her, beside her, surrounding her, protecting her. We're used to her sudden tears which can come at any moment, just before lunch, or out on our mountain walk yesterday.

We need to go in around five-fifteen she says. It'll be just after dark and any friends will probably be out on the streets, busking, scoring or stealing. The driver wants to do a dry run first so we can all get our bearings. This'll take about half an hour. It takes about forty minutes to get from here to there so we need to leave at three-thirty. Time for a quick game of dominoes. Maltese Cross.

It's over quickly. Astrid wins. Maria fed her all the doubles and she had the right follow-ups. Big Pete loses. "He's a bad loser" says Maria. "That'll wind him up."

It's twenty past two. We've got ten minutes. I'm Swiss when it comes to timing. We'll leave on the dot. We all light up cigarettes and sit in silence as the minute hand creeps down.

At twenty nine minutes past, the driver turns to Big Pete.

"Whatever you do, don't kill him, otherwise we'll all be fucked. Let's go and have a coffee at the bar and get on with it."

It's raining outside. Perfect. Keep the spectators at home. On the other hand it could mean we'll have more to contend with. Too bad. Six of one.

Astrid and Maria have a brandy each, Pete and I coffee. Then we're really on our way. Pete's chosen the music. James Brown. As we stop at the lights there's a funeral procession in the rain opposite.

Green and we go.

8

Evenings in Tuscany

Astrid came into breakfast on the second morning after she got back from her honeymoon in Perugia and asked what I had been writing about. I told her the various chapters, what they were called at the moment, mentally checking through my documents in Rings Around the Moon, the working title I used then. She asked me if she was in the book and I said she wasn't, which was true. She knew I'd been writing about her and I didn't pretend I hadn't, but joked that she was an ongoing story, whereas 'my book' ended with Saint Francis and Leonardo da Vinci, long before I ever met her.

She then told me about the dream she'd had the night before. She dreamt I had a chapter called Penny Whistles which started off with a fanfare of trumpets. I said I'd forgotten, there was a file called Penny Whistles but there was nothing in it yet; it was one of a few that were titles with some notes to follow up. She laughed, and with her mouth full of scrambled egg, she said:

"You can write my story if you want. I give you complete freedom. Someone's got to write it and I would rather it was you."

The first I heard that she might be coming back here again was when she called me one night nearly two weeks ago.

"Martin, I'm afraid. He's going to kill me. He's insanely jealous and his heroin addiction is driving me crazy. I love him but I'm so frightened."

I could hear the faint sound of traffic in the background and pictured her in a public phone booth looking warily out through the glass as she spoke.

"I don't want to go back to the States you know that. I'll just become a weapon in my parents' fucked up war."

She was crying now. I told her she could always come to my house and I could drive over and collect her.

"No. It's too dangerous. I'll find my own way to you."

Then her voice dropped to a whisper.

"I've got to hang up. I must go.... "

Gone.

Great! Just when my life seemed to have settled down into a normal rhythm again, back comes Astrid!

Her father had called me early September saying she'd taken off from San Francisco and gone to live with a heroin addicted rock musician in Perugia. The former headmaster of the school in Arezzo sensitively repeated this out loud to everyone in the bar in Cortona where I was sitting as he was fumbling around restructuring his career. I'd technically written Astrid out of the equation of my life. Heroin and friends linked to heroin was the worst news, a dead end for all involved. I knew that from the past.

Then her father called again a few weeks later and asked if I could go over to Perugia and see if his daughter was OK. I'd been once before, off my own bat, but it was like searching for a needle in a haystack. This time her father had some leads, the name of a park where she'd hung out and several receipts from some bar, the Bar Alibi.

I called Rosemary who had worked at the school and knew Astrid. She lived near Perugia. She agreed to help me. It would be much easier working as a pair. Alone it would be hopeless and depressing. Together we would be our own witnesses.

We met on a Saturday at five on a warm October evening at the bar where I used to meet Astrid in the summer. Just on the off chance I showed the barman some photos of her. Yes, he'd seen her quite often and recently, but if we called in again around seven, his son would be back and he'd know for sure where she hung out.

We drove to the park as there was about an hour of daylight left. It was on a hill just outside the city and was one of the most gloomy and evil places I've ever been to. It had airs of being a picnic and recreational park with play areas, climbing frames and barbeque grills where parents might have taken their children once, but the place was run down, rusting, rotten and litter-strewn. There were groups of young men sitting around on dilapidated benches amongst litter, passing joints between them and looking suspiciously at Rosemary. We must have looked like two parents looking for their child, which was almost true. The eyes that watched us must have seen couples like us often. Rosemary kept up my spirits by telling me how she and her first husband used to get up in disguises and follow their son around the streets as he was an uncontrollable minor under the influence of another, older man. As if I hadn't heard these stories before. She told me that she'd tried to contact him the last time she was back in the States but he refused to see her. I couldn't imagine having that non-relationship with my daughter. Rosemary was for scouring the woods, but the place was getting to me, bringing me down, and I urged her that we quit and go try the Alibi bar in the city. We drove back and I parked in the little piazza where I used to collect Astrid for the weekends during the summer and where she cried and lied to me about going back to the States.

We walked past Astrid's old apartment in better days, past the school where she'd studied, up through the Etruscan arch and into the old city with its narrow medieval streets. It didn't take long to find the Alibi bar. It was tiny and off the edge of a long narrow piazza in the city centre. There were about ten people inside and it seemed packed. We went in, squeezed up to the bar and I ordered a couple of drinks, a Campari for Rosemary and acqua minerale for myself. I stood facing Rosemary who had a view into the bar. Mine was out onto the dark street.

"She's here!" she said excitedly.

My heart stopped and my hand started shaking. I'd never expected we'd find her so easily. After a cigarette to calm down, I turned round and saw her down at the far end of the bar, chatting to an old man and a young lady about her own age. She looked great and I'm sure she'd seen us and was acting out she hadn't. I finished my cigarette and drink and told Rosemary I was going over to speak with her. I edged my way through the two deep crowd in the narrow bar and saw Astrid's face in the mirror on the wall. I reached across and tapped her on the shoulder.

"Hi Astrid."

She looked surprised, then shocked and came across towards me as I retreated back to Rosemary.

"We just came to see if all's well; if you're OK."

She said it was such a surprise to see us, she never expected it. She had tears in her eyes as she pulled us over to meet her boyfriend, a dark skinned man of indeterminable age (I knew he was in his thirty somethings) with long black hair tied back in a pony tail. He had a finely chiselled handsome face and wore a yellow shirt. As Astrid introduced us, he pulled its long sleeves down to his wrists. I shook his hand and he looked like he wanted to knife me there and then. I asked Astrid if I could speak to her alone and left her talking to him as Rosemary and I went back to the entrance of the bar and watched. He seemed to take some persuading, but Astrid is persuasive and she disappeared briefly and came back with a black leather jacket and suddenly we were all three outside in the city street night lights. I put my arm around her shoulder.

"Hey it's good to see you again. You look great."

She started to cry.

Rosemary said "You'd probably like to be alone. I'll go back into the bar and talk to him."

What a professional! Keep him in sight.

"It's probably not your kind of bar" Astrid warned.

"I can handle that" Rosemary replied as she turned and went back into the bar.

We walked up the street with Astrid really blubbing now, crossed the piazza and sat on the steps outside the cathedral. I asked if she had cigarettes and she said money for them was a problem so we crossed the street to a tobacco shop and I bought her a pack of reds and told her to choose a lighter when she said hers had been stolen. Back on the steps she told me she was OK. Living in a squat. Free electricity, one meal a day. She was planning to go north to pick apples where she'd heard she could earn good money. She hadn't called me as she didn't want to involve me in the shit with her parents. Looking for signs of heroin, I noticed she still had her silver bracelet I'd given her in the summer.

"And the anklet," she said proudly lifting the hem of her jeans.

She looked washed and clean, healthy. I commented on her leather jacket and she said it had fallen off the back of a truck. She asked me about my life, my daughter, the kittens, the house, the work. She said she played the penny whistle tunes I'd taught her, on the streets and in a good day earned 40.000 lire or more. I'd taught her a life skill she said. What tunes did she play?

"The only two you taught me then I move to another spot."

I told her I would tell her father that I'd seen her and that she was well and if she ever needed me, all she had to do was call. She said she'd call me anyway, even if she didn't need to and now she should be getting back.

Rosemary was in conversation with Kazim and Astrid introduced me to a Scotsman who took an instant dislike to me because I spoke a different English than he. I tried not to sound patronizing but couldn't wait to get out and home. A family of Turks or Moroccans came in and Astrid's boyfriend took one of the children onto his knee. Family man. Kids love him. Time to go.

Rosemary and I said goodbye to the yellow shirted guy with the dark ponytail, the Scotsman and a drunk old man who was complaining about the price of a glass of wine. I kissed Astrid on both cheeks earning another thousand slow deaths from her lover and we left. Rosemary asked if I wanted to come back to her place for a meal but I was beat and wanted to get home. After some questions about Astrid's friend, his problems and how much lay-off pay we were still due from the old school, I thanked her and drove home.

I called Astrid's father in San Francisco and told him that his daughter seemed to be fine and in good shape. She didn't seem to be on heroin and probably the best thing was to leave her alone for the time being.

That's it I thought. Now I could get on with my life, but there was always Astrid, especially at nights when the lights of the Umbrian capital lit up the clouds over the hills to the south east of my little stone house.

Five weeks after I saw her, I got that tearful phone call about love and death.

Her father called me and told me he'd heard from her and she wanted to get out and would be coming to me for a few days then going back to the States. I got her room ready and waited, the worst job in the world, waiting, especially for her.

I waited a week. Then Rosemary called in the evening to say Astrid was on the train, on her way. I drove to the station but she wasn't there. I'd missed the train so raced back up to town and came up behind the bus. She must be on it. The bus pulled into the piazza and stopped. There was one passenger. Her. As the door opened, I reached up and took her bag and carried it across to my car and put it in the back. She turned to look at me and started crying.

"Time for a drink," I said. She agreed but first needed a pack of reds. She sat in the bar sipping her pinot looking pale and thin, even in her winter clothes.

"I might be pregnant."

Here we go. I didn't tell her I hoped she wasn't but just asked how she felt about that.

"Well, it'll be mine," she smiled.

After she'd smoked three cigarettes right down

to the filters and downed another drink, we drove up into the hills to my house and I ran her a bath.

Washed and fresh she told me about the bath she'd had at Rosemary's the night before, the dirt that came off her. Tonight's was a hot rinse. All I could think about was that she was safe and now was the time to use the lessons learnt with a lady called Scarlet, fifteen years earlier. There were so many coincidences. A nineteen year old, fair haired girl involved with a heroin addict in the same city. Scarlet was shooting up and she'd come here and dump her syringes into the woodstove. She'd stay for a few days, then she was off again. There was no stopping her.

After dinner, I asked Astrid a question:

"Have you been using heroin?"

I had a plan to strip her naked except for her knickers and search every inch of her body. She read my mind:

"You can strip me naked and search every inch of my body if you want to be sure."

"OK. I trust you. But where's the silver bracelet?"

"I traded it for a pair of leg warmers in Bologna. It was bitterly cold."

She showed me the anklet. Still there. Lucky ankle.

"I nearly lost that several times but I cast a spell on it and always got it back."

For what? I thought.

That first night, we stayed up until two in the morning as she began to tell me about the last three months in her life.

She'd left the States ten days after she arrived back

there. She'd sold her terracotta head, the one she stole from the villa in Arezzo and painstakingly restored. To make up her fare she forged a cheque of her dad's to pay for the ticket, gone back to Perugia to be with the guy who'd kept her high the last three weeks of the summer. Her father called me to say she'd taken off and a few days after that he called again saying Astrid had called her mother and was back in Italy living with a thirty six year old Turk who was a heroin addict.

Now, sipping red wine and smoking a cigarette as she sat by the woodstove in my living room looking all scrubbed and clean she brought me up to date:

"No one told me about heroin, what colour it was, how people shot up, what it did to them," she said.

"By the time I knew he was an addict it was too late. Then I just thought what the hell. I can't go back so this is the only way. When you came to look for me with Rosemary, it was too early. The beatings hadn't started. I still had all my possessions. I was healthy and earning money playing the penny whistles. After the first few weeks he stopped bringing me coffee in bed in the mornings. Then the beatings started. He slapped me around the face several times. He started to threaten me:

"'My God will never forgive' you he'd yell."

She didn't tell me for what his God wouldn't forgive her for. Even if she knew.

"Then, one night, in front of his friends, he pulled me down the iron spiral staircase by my hair. As he was about to punch me I saw an empty Cheres beer bottle and managed to grab it and hit him over the head with it, hard. Another time, in the street, he started to hit me around the head and the local police intervened and started to kick him only I stopped them saying it was all OK. It was my fault. I was emotionally upset. Then he got hold of my arm and led me back home where he really started to hit me. I could see another one coming. He pulled my head towards him by my hair and wham! He had this bamboo stick he'd keep on the kitchen table and he held me down and beat my ribs with it."

She showed me the stick in one of her blurred photographs.

"He was always short of money. I earned well playing the penny whistles and we went to the vegetable market in the evenings and were given the leftovers. But he was always shooting up even after he got his methadone from the hospital. I was told to keep out of my bedroom. My bedroom! I once went in and there they were, he and his friends, fixing. My possessions started to disappear, one by one. My walkman. My camera, though I got it back again. Your silver bracelet and anklet nearly went. He said I was selfish keeping them. Then he said I should hook for him. He knew an old man who would pay enough for an hour with me, so finally I decided to call his bluff. I agreed I'd go with this old guy and we went to find the house and rang the bell but there was no reply so I asked where the next client was and we set off, me walking in front of him. Suddenly I felt a blinding pain across my face and I collapsed to the ground blood pouring out of my head. He'd hit me right across my nose without any warning. I didn't even see it coming.

He cried, apologizing and took me home and washed my face. There's a chip in the bone in my nose. Here, put your finger there. Can you feel a dent? I had two black eyes for days, so large that even my dark glasses couldn't hide them. Our friends in the bar looked away when they saw me and when they did ask what had happened I told them I'd fallen down the stairs, but they knew. That beating is why I can't walk in front of you in the street, why I won't let you open doors for me to let me go in first and I really miss those courtesies but I'm too scared. After another incident, he nearly broke my fingers. He grabbed my hands and bent them back until I screamed and I couldn't play the penny whistles for days. Another time he held me up by my neck, hanging me, choking me so I could hardly breathe."

"But he kept me high. This was the first attraction to him back in the summer when Mojo, a mutual friend, introduced us: getting high. He always scored without any hassles. No hanging around waiting at bars and corners. He just came out with it. Then he kissed me and I started to love him."

"There was never a day without hash, ecstasy, speed (free like his methadone from the hospital) and cocaine on my birthday. Once, one of his friends put three tabs of acid into my mouth. Alcohol too. I could drink anybody under the table. I could handle eight Cheres beers in a row and once, I started the day, or rather the evening, as our days started in the evenings, with five brandies and walked away from the bar unscathed. He tried to sell me to a Turkish friend of his. If I'd marry this guy to get him American citizenship, he'd pay us two million lire. I finally knew I had to get out when he started to make plans for me to go to Turkey to see his relatives. He wanted to trade my return ticket to the States for a ticket to Istanbul. That's when I got really scared."

Those first evenings with Astrid back were filled with these monologues. I didn't have to ask questions. It just came pouring out with occasional breaks for meals, tears or games of dominoes.

"Oh, the dommies are great" she said. "Light relief."

And the wine, food and hot baths. Fed, bathed and refreshed, she'd continue:

"I learnt the street life. How to walk watching the ground for anything to pick up. Cigarettes half smoked. No wonder I smoke right down to the filters. Every last drop. I learnt a lot though. I learnt to share the little I had with the other street people, to give away my last cigarette."

"Money was always short. I tried to keep my penny whistle earnings for myself, but then he got jealous because I was out on the streets on my own earning, so he decided we could make good money selling roasted chestnuts, and friends helped us make a push-able grill using an old wheel chair and half an oil drum. We bought our first chestnuts on credit from a man in the vegetable market where we went to scavenge for damaged vegetables for our meals. I wheeled the grill up the hill to the centre of town and I can tell you Martin, that was tough going, apart from cutting the chestnuts with a knife before they went on the grill. Look. My thumbs are still scarred from doing that.

But we made up to 200.000 lire a night selling two sized packs, one for 3.000 lire and another for 5.000 lire. We were undercutting the competition and were finally ordered to quit by the local police. We never paid for our last consignment of chestnuts."

"One night, we stole a Fiat 5OO, a cinquecento, like yours outside. We drove to a suburb on the outskirts of the city and broke into this villa he'd been told about but found only liquor, no food, so what we couldn't drink there we took back with us then ditched the chink."

She pulled out her book of pathetic photographs and showed me out-of-focus shots of a plate of eggs she'd taken while she was out of her mind on an acid trip; a portrait of her in her stolen, hip clinging jeans; blurred portraits of drunken old men, and a photo of a tramp, the only good picture in the plastic folder.

"This is my wedding photograph."

She leant across and handed me her battered album.

"We got married in a ceremony in the little mad house and invited our friends in to have a party."

She pointed out and named the two rows of laughing faces with herself in the centre dressed in her green lacy dress, the one she'd worn the day we went to a boring private view of a local painter's pictures the previous summer, hours before she changed into shorts and a T-shirt and we went off and robbed the villa in Arezzo.

I told her I was invited to Thanksgiving dinner the next day. She could come too. Another Thanksgiving with Astrid, our third. I was invited to the house of the former headmaster and his wife to celebrate with turkey and pumpkin pie. When I called them up and said Astrid was staying so could I bring her too, the former headmaster said there wasn't space so I said I couldn't come as I wasn't going to leave her at my house alone. He called back later and said they would make the extra space so we went together. Before dinner we gave thanks in turn for different reasons and she gave thanks to her guardian angels. I wondered who the others were.

On the way home she went very quiet. When I asked her why, she said it was all those road signs pointing to Perugia.

We stopped off at Big Pete and Maria's. Pete promised to fix the brakes on my car and had forgotten our appointment and I wanted to make another. I introduced them to Astrid and we fixed for lunchtime on the Saturday.

We'd hardly got home and inside when she burst into tears. I sat in the armchair and she sat on my lap sobbing like a child, shuddering to a halt to blow her nose often, until I had to lift her up, sit her in the chair and get more tissues from the kitchen. I sat down on a chair opposite her as she blew, wiped, blew again and mopped herself up. I poured her a glass of wine and lit her a cigarette.

"Thanks. Fuck, where he hit me on my nose hurts when I cry, but I feel better. Is it red?"

She laughed, her eyes glistening in the light like a garden in the sunshine after rain. Then as if she'd thrown a switch, her expression changed and she came out with her plan.

"I want to go back to Perugia. I have to go back. I want to collect the stuff I left behind and I want to do something else. I want to hurt him. Really hurt him. I'll never be able to wipe out the pain he gave me, but I want him to feel pain now so I won't feel it any more. I want to hurt his body and even more, I want to hurt his pride. You know how proud he is of his pony-tail? He told me he could have any woman in town because of his hair. Well I want to cut it off and I want to scar his face for life so everytime he looks in the mirror he'll remember me and what he did to me. Every time he's with another woman she'll ask what happened to him, how he got that scar and he'll remember. I want him never to forget me. I don't want to kill him though, that would be too quick. I want him to live with his pain for the rest of his life."

"We'll need some help," I said, automatically including myself in her plan.

"Oh, you're not coming. I'm not going to get you into all this shit."

"I'm already in this shit Astrid and, anyway, you'll need a driver. We have to find the right people to help."

She suggested Rosemary but I knew she wouldn't agree with the plan.

She then suggested a couple we knew, a lady who had worked at the school and her Italian boyfriend.

"They won't do it," I said. "Anyway, they're too close to us and would be immediate suspects if anything goes wrong. We'll come up with somebody. Listen, I want you to write down everything he did to you and everything you want to do to him."

She sat at my desk and in her daisy chain handwriting she compiled two lists. When she was done, I read out loud the items in each list one by one as if we were planning a long camping holiday which is probably what we would have had to do if she had carried out half of what was on the second list and were caught.

When she finished she handed me the list and I put it in a safe place as an insurance policy.

"I'm an alcoholic and a drug addict," she said. She'd brought some bed covers up from her bedroom and made a nest on the couch. Her voice came from beneath the covers.

"Shh. Go to sleep. It's late and you're exhausted."

"When you went out of the room earlier I poured my self three glasses of wine and gulped them down. I'm a lush, like my mom."

"You're tired. Go to sleep. Good night."

On the Saturday morning after Thanksgiving we went to Big Pete and Maria's as arranged. Astrid can be captivating, bewitching. She can charm the pants off anyone, female as well as male, if she sets about it. I left her with Maria in their tiny kitchen while Big Pete and I repaired the brake pads on the car and, by the time we'd finished and washed up, she'd told a version of her story to Maria and had her completely spellbound. As Big Pete and I sat down with them to eat, Astrid turned to me.

"Shall we ask them to help?"

"Help what?" asked Maria.

"We'll tell you soon."

After lunch and the inevitable game of dommies

we arranged to meet that evening for a pizza up at a restaurant in the hills near to my house.

"We'll tell you tonight."

That night sitting at a large table in the restaurant with some Italian friends of our friends, Maria, wide eyed, turned to Pete:

"Pete! Do you understand what they're asking us to do? What you've got to do?"

Pete was eating the second half of my pizza and would eat what Astrid left when she'd done.

"Yeah. I hold him down while you collect Astrid's stuff then give him a short back and sides with a close shave."

"Christ, he will too. I know him. Once he gets involved he's a killer." Maria's face glowed.

"Pete, you're not to kill him, understand!" I was clear.

They hadn't needed much persuading. They'd taken a shine to Astrid and were convinced of the justice of her cause, even if it was a bit summary and vigilantesque to say the least.

On Sunday after roast beef, roast potatoes, brussels sprouts and Yorkshire pudding with gravy, the first time I'd eaten that traditional English meal in over twenty years, we went for a walk along the Roman road in the hills going through the fine details of our plans. I was glad I was on Astrid's side and that Big Pete was on the same side and glad too Maria was going to be there to keep Astrid's mind on her job so Big Pete could do his. We were a good team. We didn't come better.

We decided to go for it the next evening, Monday, and get it over with as soon as possible.

9

Nightlife in Umbria

We're approaching Perugia and the rain is coming down harder. The car feels like it's going to aquaplane so I slow down crossing the long viaduct. The towers, domes and spires are just visible in the twilight, up on the hill through the rain. We turn off the highway before the first of the tunnels and down onto the old road where the Albanian and Nigerian girls stand waiting, where I expected to find Astrid one evening in a nightmare, if she'd stayed on. There's a blonde girl, her height and age, standing under an umbrella in high, black boots, a mini-skirt, black leather jacket like Astrid's, the one she picked up in the street.

It's always a bitch getting into Perugia. The number of times I've aimed for somewhere and ended up on my way to Rome or Assisi or somewhere else. It's all four-lane one-ways. Last summer, going to collect

Astrid, I finished up in an underground car park. This time is going to be different. No mistakes.

The traffic has thickened. It's the evening rush hour. Just before the train station, the car in front brakes hard and I slam on mine. The tyres are bad, nearly bald, but we stop in time.

"Good brakes" says Pete.

We climb the hill towards the old walls and stop at the lights outside the gate. Refugees from Bosnia are out begging. If the first driver gives then the rest give. The beggars know this. If the first driver shakes his head and winds up his window, the beggar will give up after three cars. Street life goes on, rain or shine.

Green light and we go right. On, up the hill past the multi-storey car park, and approach the turnoff for the tunnel. Astrid, sitting in the back with Maria, asks for a change of music. Dylan please. Hard Rain. The best live album. He holds the notes the longest ever. This is meant to be a dry run.

"It's stopped raining" Pete says.

"We're in the tunnel, stupid." Maria says. Astrid laughs.

There's dense traffic and we're crawling behind a yellow bus and the diesel fumes are building up. Someone in the applauding crowd at the Dylan concert is yelling for 'Lay lady, lay', but just as Dylan is about to start Oh sister, when I come to lie in your arms, we're out of the tunnel and I cut the music.

"Astrid! Where are we? Directions!"

"Straight on," she says! "OK. Further. Yes, a bit more. There it is! That's the house."

It's red. The *vino novello* red the Italian State

paints the *ANAS* houses, once the homes of the road maintainers. Went with the job. It's got a smudge of neo-classical about it. Late nineteenth century. If it had been in Britain it would have been neo-gothic. Its lower walls are covered with graffiti and shreds of posters and the louvered shutters are closed. I pull over to the right and slip between the parked cars. They're everywhere! No way are we getting ourselves blocked in here.

We go past and pull over and let Big Pete go and check the place out.

"Do you want the umbrella?"

He ignores the question.

"He's oblivious to cold and wet" says Maria, and we wait.

So this is where Astrid's been hanging out the last three months. While I've been three hills away trying to write a book and put her out of my mind, she's been here, in a mad house with a mad man. She loved him. She loves him and here we are, under her directions, following her instructions, just about to give him something to remember her by for the rest of his life. Hope he's home. Without the dogs. Alone.

Pete comes back, striding through the drizzle and gets in. He doesn't seem to need to say a thing, so I guess he's happy with the layout as I turn the car and we ease through the spaces left between parked cars, back past the little red house. I get a better look at the entrance this time. That's where Astrid went in and out, right on the main road. Her house. The noise. As we pull out into the traffic there's a bus stop on the right, ten metres on from the house. Good place to park next time around.

Now we're going over the getaway route.

"Straight on at the lights" says Astrid "and through the arch."

She drew it on her map. She was in my cartography class at school. Then we're into a narrow street inside the walls and suddenly I recognize where we are. There's the Etruscan gate on our left with its scars and cracks from time and earthquakes; the bar, where Astrid and I exchanged bad news back in the summer. There's the narrow road to the house where she lived before all this happened, where the wing mirror of a passing bus could remove your sunglasses if you weren't careful walking out of her door. We turn down before it and come out by the gate where we started. Time to go shopping.

Astrid and Maria get out at the multi-storey car park. They're going to buy a can of spray paint. Black paint. Pete and I sit under the tapping rain and I ask him to choose the music. Madame Butterfly. He surprises me. It's about a quarter of an hour from the wet run. We're half way through the Humming Chorus when the ladies get back, laughing. Astrid holds up her little paper bag.

One more bar stop. Somewhere we've never been before and where we're never likely to go again. Big Pete and I have coffees. Astrid and Maria brandies. I'm surprised Astrid doesn't want to pee. She's usually dying to, bursting after an hour. I go and so does Pete. I pay and hope the barman forgets our faces. It's five exactly. We're right on time.

Back up the hill to the tunnel. Traffic's as thick as the night and it's raining hard. There's a short queue waiting to turn into the tunnel and traffic inside is stalled. Minutes. Seems like weeks. Then we're across and stuck in the entrance with not quite enough rain for the wipers. Crawl. Stop. Crawl. Stop. It takes a lifetime. Some cars in front give up, do a left U-turn and we inch forward. Just have to sit this out. We can't change plans now. No music. Not even Astrid wants music. Everyone's silent, concentrating, focussed. What a team! I'd hire us if ever I needed to do a job like this again.

Then we're out into the rain again. I let a surprised lady walk across the white stripes in front of us. English politeness. We turn, go down and the house is still there. I pass it and pull into the bus stop. An Alfa pulls out in front as if part of the plan and I take its place leaving plenty of room behind for buses and the other entrance to the car park clear in front.

We get out and I remove Astrid's empty black bag from the boot and give it to her with a hug and a kiss. I kiss Maria too and say *bon lavoro* and they follow Big Pete into the darkness. I'd have kissed him too except he'd probably have thumped me. Anyway, he's gone. They've gone. It's five twenty exactly.

I get back into the car and find the Remmy Ongala tape. Tanzania. Kenya. I want to go home. Getaway music. The rear wiper's giving me a view of a rubbish container and a few people waiting at the bus stop under yellow lights. Others walk past under umbrellas. A lady stops impatiently as her dog takes a shit, its coat glistening. The traffic on the left is building up into a jam. A yellow bus, blazing like a Christmas tree pulls in behind and can't get back out into the marmalade of trucks and cars. A police car pulls alongside, blue lights circling, glittering off wet metal. Not already! How did they know? Then it moves on in the sluggish flow. A car pulls in front trying to get into the car park but it's too crowded so it backs out, blocking my getaway until a kind taxi lets it through. I wipe the rear windscreen. It's still got Maria's hand marks on the inside where she wiped it earlier. I check the time. Five twenty nine. I imagine another twenty minutes. I waaaaaanta goooo hoooooome.

Suddenly Astrid's at the back of the car carrying a pile of black boxes. I jump out and open up the fifth door for her. She's breathing hard and Maria's right behind her carrying the bag. I bundle that in too and close the door. They get in the back.

"Where's Pete?" Maria shouts.

"If he doesn't get here quick, we're leaving and we'll meet him later on the cathedral steps as we agreed." I'm in command.

"No! He's coming! The guy's chasing him!" Astrid shouts and tries to get out but I get out quicker and close her door. Pete's walking back towards a bus that's just pulled in. He turns and strides back to the car. He's in, but I can't pull out as the bus is blocking me.

"He's on the bus!" shouts Astrid.

Shit! The bus moves off and I pull out behind it. The bastard's going to jump off and try and get us. I press down the button on my door locking us all in.

"No, he's going to the hospital. That bus goes to

the hospital. Keep to the left and go straight at the lights. The bus will turn off."

Astrid leans over from the back and hands Big Pete a huge knife.

"Always wanted one of these," he says, "but I've got to get rid of this one first."

He's got a bloody Stanley knife in his hand.

We crawl through another traffic jam and I resist the temptation to turn down side roads every time things get snarled up. Two buses are squaring off outside a church, but cars are getting through, half up on the narrow pavement. Then it clears and we pass the Etruscan gate and drive right up into the centre of the city. Astrid has a message to deliver and has to pay a bar bill. The three get out behind the cathedral and I turn the car and wait outside a food shop with the engine running, imagining that the customers are taking down the number plate and my description, so I open the sunroof to let in a little rain as it's like an oven inside.

My God! They took nine minutes to do that, whatever they did! Pete's got a bloody cutter so he did something and Astrid got the stereo and her stuff. I can't wait to hear it all. They'll probably all talk at once.

They're back again! God these guys are fast! We're off down the narrow one ways, wet cobbles, slippery hairpin bends. I've never been this way before so follow the signs to Roma and Firenze.

There are a few minutes silence. Big Pete sits back quietly in the front seat, telling me if it's clear to the right on the sharper bends.

Then they start talking.

Astrid first:

"I saw Giovanna and paid her. Michael was in the bar too. I told him justice was done."

Then it all comes out:

"Pete, that's incredible! I've never seen you listen to anyone else on a job before but when Astrid shouted at you to turn his head, you twisted it up for her. I was shouting at you to get a move on Astrid and you were happily spraying messages all over the walls.

Then you sprayed his face."

"I managed to spray half of it. I kicked him twice. In the balls. Fuck, my foot hurts." Astrid laughs.

"You hit him on the head too."

"So did you. You were screaming at him. Dirty Coward. Beating women."

"What did you spray on the walls?" I ask.

"BASTARD! and I BEAT WOMEN! And GOD WILL NEVER FORGIVE YOU. That's what he always said to me. GOD WILL NEVER FORGIVE YOU."

"When we were upstairs I could hear Pete saying, I thought I told you to stay on the ground. Then thump!"

"He was screaming, shouting. Asty! I love you! I did everything for you! Why are you doing this to me? He should bloody well know why."

"There was no one there in the house with him. Even the dogs were out." We never even thought of that possibility.

"Did you manage to cut off his ponytail Pete?"

"Most of it."

"And you got rid of the knife?"

"Yeah. Dumped it in a waste bin in town."

"Did you cut him?"

"Yeah," and he draws a line down his cheek with his finger like a Roman saying the food was delicious.

"That's why he jumped straight on a bus to the hospital."

"I thought he was trying to get away and the bus just happened to pull in so he jumped on."

"He had to get to the hospital after what Pete did to him. Did you see those punches he was giving him in the back. God he must have looked a sight on the bus. Can you imagine? Bleeding and half his face black."

"I cut his back up too. Lucky it was only a Stanley knife and not this thing though this is as blunt as my arse."

"Did you get all your stuff Astrid?" I cut in.

"Most of it. I was trying to unhook the stereo when the whole kitchen bar tipped over. I must have pushed it. I couldn't get the wires undone so I just pulled them out. We left the speaker."

Then they're quiet again and I turn up Remmy Ongala. He's still wanting to go home. I agree.

We're out on the highway and suddenly Astrid bursts into tears and sobs into Maria's embrace. Maria tries to soothe her and calm her with words.

"You did the right thing. He deserved it. Remember what he did to you. Never forget all the terrible things he did to you." She's reassuring.

"I'm going to turn off by the lake. There's a bar there I know, and this time, we're all having brandies."

Astrid's stopped crying when we get out. She's

limping. Maria's got her arm around her and I give her a hug.

It's normal inside the bar, warm and we're nobodies again. They sit at a table and I order four brandies please.

"OK. Tell me from the beginning."

Astrid starts.

"His key was in the door so I knew he was at home. I knocked and he came out onto the balcony, looked down and said who's there? He saw me. Pete and Maria were hiding round the corner. He opened the door and he had his arms outstretched, greeting, welcoming me. He must have thought I was coming back to him. Then, as he gave me a hug, Maria walked in."

"You should have seen the look on his face when I came through the door! There he was hugging you and suddenly I walk in!"

"Maria walked by me then Pete came in right behind her and the next minute, I felt myself being pulled to the floor as Pete dragged him down. Maria pulled me away and we were off upstairs and left him with Pete. Oh, I got the knife from its hiding place first and put it in my back pocket. We were fast. The pile of clothes was in the corner of the bedroom and I pulled mine out. I couldn't find my good pair of jeans though. I could hear him screaming from down below and Maria kept shouting at me not to listen to him as she was bundling my things into the bag. We went into the other room and I got my books, had another quick look for my jeans then we were back downstairs again getting the stereo. He was really howling then. I took out the spray and started on the walls. At first it didn't come black but after a few seconds it came out really well. I sprayed it right across one wall, large. GOD WILL NEVER FORGIVE YOU. When I'd finished, I went over to him and shouted 'Wanna a fix then? Wanna fix?' And I hit him twice on the head. Then Pete twisted his head up and I sprayed half of his face and screamed 'You bastard!' Then I kicked him twice in the balls but I must have got something else as my foot's really killing me. Then Maria and I rushed out and we left him with Pete."

"Pete, he followed you out," says Maria.

"Yeah, but I turned round to get him and he jumped on the bus."

"When I saw him coming after you," says Astrid, "I was going to get out and help you. I pulled the knife out. Then you got into the car."

I order another four brandies.

Then I fish in my pocket for the keys to the *cinquecento*, my little yellow car that got me out of so many scrapes over the years but was now sitting at home, unused, rusting. I put the keys on the table and tell Pete and Maria that is their pay for the evening's work. Maria protests but I insist.

"I got given tonight's car for helping someone so you get one too. Come on, drink up and let's go home. I'm beat."

We drop them off at their place, turning down an offer of tea. I want to get home. Astrid says she needs a hot bath. We'll call them tomorrow.

Back in the hills, I park the car right outside the house on the apology of a lawn so we don't have to carry her stuff far. When we get inside, Astrid flops down in the armchair and bursts into tears.

10

Glasses of Hours

Today is International AIDS Day and I woke Astrid up early. Today she has her AIDS test and it's also her dad's birthday. What a great way for her to start today.

She's been through it all before though, after her escapade with Jack, her kidnapper, and knows it means more people sticking more things into her body which is why she's not her usual self at breakfast.

I bought her a decent pair of boots last night before we went to see Patrizia, the doctor, to get the necessary papers and she said she felt better with good leather underfoot but it should have been her dad's job to buy her boots. Well he's not here to do it.

Patrizia explained that Astrid can get her test but a full medical examination has to wait until she knows if she's pregnant or not. If she's HIV positive and pregnant then she must have an abortion. What if the first test is negative and the second positive? Patrizia said let's get one result at a time and she fills out a form. I asked what I owed and she waved me away with a smile. We got in before surgery hours began.

I've learnt I can't let Astrid be on her own for a second. If she's not with me, there has to be someone I trust with her. If I go to the bathroom I worry that when I get out she'll have taken off or she's been at the wine bottle. As soon as I left the house to collect wood from the woodpile, quick as lightning she was on the phone calling one of her friends in Perugia to find out how Kazim was. When I got in, she was sitting calmly in the armchair telling me he was in hospital in a bad way. Scarred for life it seems. At least he wasn't dead I thought. Big Pete did an even better job than we thought. Then she got worried that she was going to go to jail for attempted murder. I reassured her that they weren't after us. They would have arrested us when we were stopped in the road block at the pass the morning after the job but they let us go. But I insisted she ask me before she used the phone again.

She came back from staying with a friend yesterday. I thought she needed to be with a woman and better still, a woman with a baby to get herself out of herself but it didn't work out. She'd got quieter and quieter as we drove over to their house on the hill and when I left her, she started crying. I called her that night and she sounded lonely and isolated. But she'd tested herself with a pregnancy kit twice and was negative both times. I called her again the next night and she'd started her period. My friend said she was missing me and needed some TLC. I'd be over to collect her in the morning and take her to the hospital to get the results of her AIDS test. It had to be negative.

Coming back from my friend talking about the choices she had if it was negative she said:

"I'm not afraid of death Martin. I'm afraid of life. Life - piece of shit. Death - piece of cake."

I told her I valued her life more than she did.

I dropped her at the hospital and parked by the ambulances as she went off with her piece of paper. Within two minutes, she appeared in the rear view mirror holding a white envelope in one hand, disappeared and reappeared life size and I open the passenger door for her, one door I can open without her being afraid.

"Negative." she said and I gave her a big hug but she was quiet, almost disappointed. Two negatives in twenty four hours.

Big Pete and Maria came for dinner and I opened a special wine to celebrate. Suddenly it dawned on Astrid she was through, clear, clean, fresh again and she cheered up. Maria invited her to go to a club with them and stay over at their place after. In the morning when I collected her she said she was so pleased to see me.

She laughed most of the day otherwise she said she'd cry. I bruised a rib repairing a woodstove and it ached from laughing with her. She spoke with Patrizia who said she really had to get to work on her relationship with her parents. Breaking free. Patrizia made a snipping gesture with her fingers.

It's time to do the Tarot cards. My suggestion. I feel the time's right. She agrees.

She relaxes, clears the hexagonal table and wipes it clean with a duster, removes the pack, shuffles it after I've made sure all the cards are the right way up. We don't want any ambiguity, at least I don't. I want as clear a reading as possible. She spreads them out into a rainbow semicircle face down, adjusting cards that are hidden to give them a fair chance of being chosen. Vanya, one of my brother's former girlfriends, taught me how to teach this way of reading and it had always proved an accurate mirror of the reader.

"Remember," Vanya said, "this is only a mirror. It will reflect what you put into it. Approach the cards carefully and with respect. If you respect them they will respect you."

Astrid relaxes, breathes deeply and slowly draws the first card, placing it face downwards on the table in front of her at twelve o'clock. Two more, one at nine o'clock and the third at three o'clock. She really takes her time choosing. She places the last and fourth card at six o'clock then turns them over one by one. She knows she should read them like pictures, just like we did in art history classes. Interpretations later. I will draw my own conclusions as we go along but keep them to myself.

These first four represent her recent past. The top card, the head card, is The Tower. Astrid's Tower. The ending of a relationship. Two figures, struck demoniacally from their tower by lightning, a crown toppling, the man and woman plunge through tear-filled sky into the abyss.

The next two cards are her heart cards. Three of Swords. Three swords pierce a heart that floats in a cloudy sky. Sorrow, heartbreak and excruciating pain as a result. Accept the pain and change it into something positive. Love? Second heart card is two of Pentacles. Astrid's laughter card, always laughing, always mysterious.

The bottom card, what she felt deep down inside her is the Devil. Friend of the Devil's a friend of mine. Male and female chained loosely to the Devil's plinth, tails on fire. Lovers before the Tower? Sensuality winning out over sense? Drugs, rape, violence? I keep quiet and let her do all the looking, reading. She's good at this, well trained on top of her natural ability.

Then she goes onto her second draw: the present.

She draws the nine of Wands, her head card. A fighter who has fought many battles, been wounded in the head and still faces more battles to come but is strong and well armed.

Next her heart cards: the first is Death. Astrid doesn't flinch. It was expected and it comes and she describes it unemotionally. Piece of cake for her. Five of Swords for her second heart card and one battle is over. Who's the winner and who are the losers? Then deep down, the Star.

The Star!! Peace after the war, rest after the turmoil. Time to gather her strength, recoup her resources. Healing. Her little creative bird chirps away in the tree behind her.

I want to say "Astrid, you couldn't have picked truer cards if you tried. They reflect what's going on with you so clearly up to this point they couldn't have been more lucid if you'd polished the mirror first." but I don't because it's time to pick the cards for the future, the future as near away from the present as the past but in the opposite direction.

She's very relaxed, not smoking even. Her eyes are half closed as she concentrates on her feelings and her hands move backwards and forwards above the cards, feeling for the pull. Then she chooses.

There is never any doubt once she's decided on a card. Two of Swords, head, eight of Swords and Temperance, heart cards, and for deep down inside her she picks the Knight of Pentacles. She combs through the images, reading all the details.

The Two of Swords: a blindfolded woman in a long, white robe sits on a stool with her back to a calm sea dotted with islands. Her arms are crossed over her breast and in each hand she holds a sword. A quarter moon looks, crescent down, at her from the sky. She'll be on the defensive, ready to strike out, yet she's more vulnerable now than before as she can't see who threatens her. Did she tie the blindfold?

The eight of Swords: a woman in an orange robe stands on slushy, wet ground. She's bound with a cloth strip and blindfolded too. Seven swords are stuck, hilts up, in a barricade behind her and another in front of her. A castle sits on a hill in the background.

There's a gap in the wall of swords through which she could step backwards and reach the castle if she could remove her bounds and blindfold.

Temperance, her second heart card: an angel stands at the edge of a pool with one foot in the water. His white robe bears an orange triangle in a white square on his breast and his golden locked forehead carries a circular clasp. His wings are outstretched. In his hands he holds two golden cups, one above and to one side of the other and water is flowing between them. To his left, a patch of irises grow and to his right, a road leads from the pool across the countryside to two distant mountains above which a golden halo shines. Temperance in the heart, emotional moderation, rehab for her feelings? Is this the other side of her, the opposite of the eight of Swords? Is this the alternative to the grey castle on the hill?

Her very last card tonight, the Knight of Pentacles: an armoured knight (unarmed?) sits on his stationary black horse. His visor is raised and he holds a single pentacle in his gloved, right hand. He looks serious, even grim. A bare landscape of rolling fields and two trees leads to distant mountains. What a disappointing card Astrid, I think, after all that you've drawn so far. I don't know what to say. It's not a card I'm familiar with.

We shut up the shop for the night and she goes to bed with the Tarot books. I'm exhausted and go up to my room. For the first night since she got back, I go to bed after her.

The next morning I told her I'd read in the newspaper a mother and two children had thrown themselves off a viaduct and she asked what a viaduct was. When I explained she said the kids were better out of it. At least they didn't have to live with fucked up parents.

Her father had called soon after she'd arrived back and after she'd spoken to him I told him she wanted to stay here for the time being and not go to his friends and then back to the States as he wanted her to, so we made a deal that she'd be left with me for the time being. When her mom called, Astrid refused to speak to her but I did. She asked if I was sleeping with her daughter! Not any more was what I didn't tell her. What a bitch we agreed afterwards.

Her grandmother faxed telling her they were all licking their wounds back home and that Astrid should get on back and pay her dues.

She spent a day and another night with Big Pete and Maria and came back the next day with her hair dyed dark reddish brown. It looked great. She wanted to go to Yorkshire and get a job to earn some money so that she could go to Scotland to be a singer and become famous. Astrid is determined to become famous. But she's worried about not being allowed back into Italy as her visa has long since expired.

I tried to get her to start learning to love herself again. Start by hating her mother. I suggested she spit in the sink each time she thought of her mother. Reduce her mother to zero. She shouldn't even waste a valuable emotion like hate on her and get on with loving herself.

That night we both had dreams about Kazim.

We stayed home the next day, hauled in wood, drank wine, played dommies and chatted. After dark, I was sitting at the table when Astrid came and sat on my lap and hugged me. As I tried to unravel her she said "I'm not letting go!" and she hung on, hugging harder. That was the longest hug I ever had. Finally she loosened her grip, dismounted and sat across from me in the armchair.

"That was a lap dance. Now I'm going to ask you some questions. Ready?"

"For what?"

"You have such a right on understanding of me. Where did you get it from?"

Floored I scratched my eyebrow.

"No, don't do that."

I rubbed my chin.

"No, answer my question."

She was using professional techniques she'd learnt at the school.

"Well....... not from my mother. Some certainly from my daughter's mum. Some from a lady friend my brother once had, a famous feminist and author."

"I thought you didn't get it from your mum. But you're bored with your book on Africa right? What were the women like in Africa?"

"Black, white and brown."

"But was there a woman there who taught you about women?"

I thought of all the women, friends' mothers and sisters, girlfriends.

"No. Not specially."

Then, for the first time in thirty two years I started to talk about the family who were more of a family to me than my family. Alex, Betty, Jenny, Trisha, little Alex and tiny Wendy.

I've thought about them regularly for all these years but never talked about them to anyone. The warmth of that almost exclusively female group. Painting, music, athletics. I was more at home in their home than mine. We were all equal. Women and men, though it was matriarchal by sheer numbers. All seven of us drove from Nairobi to Cape Town in their Citroen ID 19. Those were the days when you could do that."

"Can we make a deal?" said Astrid. "On July first next year, we go to Africa and find them, some of them, one of them. I'll be right behind you. OK?"

"You won't be behind me, you'll be beside me."

We shook hands on it.

"Another question."

"Shoot!"

"Would you ever want to get married again?"

"Jesus. I really don't know. I thought about it seriously last summer with you but I went into that with my emotional armour on. It was what you wanted. Not my idea. I guess I could never live with someone close to my own age. I don't know why but I couldn't. I'm happy on my own and have accepted it, but I keep the doors open though I feel they are closing around me."

She was leading up to something, some edge again.

"I can feel my powers coming back" she said. "Last question. Ready?"

I'm shell-shocked. This little lady has uncovered a secret in me that has lied dormant for nearly a third of a century.

"If I can't stay in Italy any other way, will you marry me? I'm frightened of going to Britain and asking someone there if I have to."

"Yes, I will." There was never any hesitation in

my reply so I quickly added "We would have to write down everything on paper first, though."

"Sure".

"It wouldn't mean that you would have to sleep with me. OK?"

"Totally."

Then, from somewhere the tears came. She'd already needed one of the longest hugs I have ever given anyone but this was more. She sat, knees up in the Astrid position, like she did in the bath last summer, like a pagan icon, a statue with all her weaknesses exposed and started crying. I went and comforted her and she slid from the chair and we fell slowly onto the floor and I held her for the longest cry she has had recently. I'd teased her earlier while she was cutting up onions and wiping away the tears that it was the first time she'd cried that day. Well, now she cried, sobbed, whimpered. She went to bed earlier than she'd done in months, and I woke her at ten the next morning. After breakfast she went straight onto the couch and fell asleep again.

Our life together is ruled by music. Time is circumscribed by music. Big Pete and Astrid have wired up the new stereo and if you sit on the steps between the kitchen and the dining room with the stove door open to get the warmth from the flames, the acoustics through the four speakers put you right in the middle of the orchestra, or the band.

"What music shall I put on?" is my most frequent question.

"Something with words." is her most frequent reply. Always something with words. As if to take her mind off her mind. Sooner or later during each day, it's The Grateful Dead. The last thing at night, usually after I've gone to bed, it's John Lennon.

We made it through the recording of the live Dead concert and Astrid became hysterical with laughter then she started crying, sobbing, whimpering like a puppy. She's a two year old in that body, an abused two year old. She eventually went to sleep on the sofa with my hands clasped in hers.

It's the same in the car. Non-stop music. Sometimes it's as if we're not living in the country and the view from the dining room windows is some animated landscape that perfectly imitates the changing light of the day over the wooded hills and the often snow covered Appenine mountains beyond and then, in those last days, it dawned on me. We were, or rather she was, back in the little red mad-house just on the edge of Perugia.

I tried to get Astrid to take some exercise as she sits around the table most of the day, talking, drinking coffee or wine and listening to music. Even Big Pete and Maria can't persuade her to come up on the Roman road again.

Once I used my sister's horse to tempt her and I had to drag her outside in her boots and up to the stable. Paddy, a large bay gelding, loved the idea and took his head collar like a lamb. I gave Astrid a leg up and took her off on a leading rein. You wouldn't think she'd been an equestrian acrobat. She rode like a beginner, a sack of flour, as I led them down to the overgrown riding school. There I let them go and Paddy burst into life and trotted around, Astrid bouncing about and clinging on. After a couple of circuits, Paddy took complete control and cantered up the hill back to his stable. If I hadn't closed the lower door he'd have gone right in, wiping Astrid off his back, but by the time I got there, puffed out, he was standing waiting for me to remove his burden. I helped Astrid dismount and led Paddy in and shut the door.

The change in Astrid was remarkable. Her face normally pale, glowed and she bounced back home with plans to do it again even on a regular basis but somehow never got round to it.

I had to twist her arm to get her to come with me up to the cemetery. I used the excuse I was researching the role of local people who'd been active in the partisan movement towards the end of the Second World War and I wanted to visit some of their graves, so Astrid grumblingly agreed to come too. We walked along the main road and round the church where the ex-nazi and nudist once lived and I'd been bitten by his Rottweiler, then on up the hill towards Amedeo's farm where the track to the *campo santo* led to the walled in cemetery.

We wandered around the sparse graves.

There was Palma, Amedeo's beautiful grandmother who died during the bitter winter of '85.

Faliero, Amedeo's father, (the local boss at whose *battiture* I'd learnt the ropes) lay beside his mum.

There was Ercole's wife whose husband had taught me to make *carbonella* and who'd narrowly escaped death by firing squad when he'd been betrayed to the Gestapo as a member of the partisans.

There was Angelone, Big Angel, the heart and

soul of the *battitura* who'd gone off the road at an S-bend on the way back from the Saturday market in his *cinquecento* five years ago and never got back on it again. The vase by the crash rail always contained fresh flowers, even in snow.

I named them all for Astrid, one after another and she listened silently.

It was a gloomy, sad and damp little space, full of memories, some mine, mostly others'.

We left and I took Astrid down a footpath to the Mission of the Faith. We scrambled through brambles and reached the fourteenth station of the cross.

Astrid was intrigued so I gave her a guided tour. She asked questions about everything she saw: the building, the statues, the well, the people who once lived here.

She was especially taken by the abandoned and rotting coach and climbed on board, sat in the mouldy driver's seat and invited me to jump on asking me if I had a valid ticket? I had to pry her away from the dump of detritus, overgrown beds, tables and desks, suppressing her scavenging instincts, saying I'd written about these people. When the school folded, I packed up my classroom, came home and wrote about the Mission of the Faith. She could read it for herself once we got home.

My sister got Astrid a job offer at the riding school where she worked, just to get her out of the house I hoped, out from under my feet, out of herself, involved with people and animals. No wages, just to work for food. I bought her a pair of green wellies for her big feet.

On her first day she was late up because it snowed during the night and only the little Renault made it up the hill. On the plain it was pouring with rain and I dropped her off wearing my raincoat and went about my business. After lunch on my way home up in the hills the snow lay so deep that I ditched my car on the pass, took out the shopping and hitched a ride with the local postman who rashly said his new car with its snow tyres could get through anything. After the pass he gave up and called a police helicopter which was wishful thinking or showing off. I got a ride with another car that lasted one more kilometre before it too ground to a halt in a drift. I walked the last kilometre with the paper shopping bag disintegrating in my arms and at the top of the drive the shopping fell about in the snow. I waded through the deep snow along the last stretch of road and down to the house where Astrid was snug and warm. I picked up a plastic bag, went back out and retrieved the shopping, got back, and she told me about her day.

She'd helped clean out the stables, brush down some horses then everyone decided to quit for the day as it was pissing down so my sister drove her home until the snow forced them to abandon the car and they'd walked the last bit, had lunch together and Astrid had made her laugh. Then she'd come on home.

She said she wanted to smoke some dope again but I thought it wasn't the right time and we had a row about it and she went off angrily to bed in the lower room even though the stove wasn't lit, instead of sleeping on the sofa which she'd made into her bed up till then.

I was invited to lunch to an interview for a new job and Astrid was invited too. She got anxious about what to wear. We planned her dress but she was getting more and more uncomfortable through the preceding day. I woke her the morning of the invitation and she said she hadn't slept for worrying about the lunch so I left her in bed and went on my own.

In the evening when I got home she'd cleaned the dining room, dresser shelves, cups and saucers, carpet, windows, the lot.

"Cleaning the outside of the windows was the only time I stepped out of the house all day."

Big Pete and Maria came for lunch Saturday and as there was still snow on the driveway, Pete pushed the Renault up the drive, lifting it up by its rear for the last few metres. After lunch we all set to it and hauled in enough wood to get through Christmas and when we were done, Astrid attacked me with a snowball and I fought back. We ended up wrestling in the snow, stuffing it down each other's jumpers. It began to get out of hand and I retreated into the house to change into dry clothes but she ambushed me so I fought back again until, finally breathless and laughing, we quit.

Maria was leaving to go back to England the next day so we said our goodbyes with hugs and plans.

When the dishes were done Astrid settled down in the armchair and began again:

"I never told you about my first skiing experience. I was twelve and my parents had taken me and my younger brother on a skiing holiday. The first morning out I went, all dressed up in my brand new gear, goggles, ski suit, lift badge. The instructor explained how to do a snow plough, turn my skis inwards to break but I couldn't get the hang of it. Then the group of us, all beginners with the instructor leading, set off down the bunny run. It was a gentle downhill beginners' slope and I started to speed up and one by one, I passed the others in the group who had all learned how to slow down, to snow plough. I slid faster and faster, calling out, as I overtook the instructor in the lead that I couldn't stop. I left the instructor and the bunnies far behind and headed out onto the serious slopes totally out of control shouting, I can't stop! I can't stop! Gathering speed, I hit a six foot ski jump, took off and in mid-air, lost one of my skiis and a pole. I landed on the remaining ski and was going even faster now, missing the ski-lift pylons and causing accidents as I crossed other skiers' paths. The slope became hard core and I was really speeding when suddenly a notice swished into view. DANGER! CLIFF AHEAD! NO SKIING BEYOND THIS POINT!. That was when I passed out and collapsed in the snow. I came round just as the instructor shook me awake and helped me back to safety. Bits and pieces of my kit were littered over a mile or more back up the slope."

"Astrid, that story is a paradigm of your life." I said.

"What's a paradigm?" she asked.

The next evening she told me she wanted to go back to Perugia.

I knew I couldn't stop her. That would mean she'd take off on her own like she did from her pa. She said she had some people to see, a bill to pay, then she'd be back. She would stay at a friend's apartment and gave me the phone number. I took her to the train station and asked her to call me the following evening. She promised she would when she got on the train and set off for the Umbrian capital.

She never called the next evening nor the following day. I called the number she'd given me. A softly spoken lady answered.

"Hello. Is Astrid there please?"

"She's not I'm afraid."

"Do you know where she is please?"

"I saw here this morning with Kazim."

"Thanks. Ciao."

Fuck. She's gone and put her head right square on the chopping block.

I called Pete.

11

Kidnapped

Pete and I make few plans as we drive through the night. We don't need to because we've done it all before. We don't discuss where we're going to look for Astrid if she isn't in the little red madhouse. I know she'll be there and that's where we're starting and Pete doesn't ask questions. I suggest that when arrive, Pete leaves the knife in the car but he puts it up his sleeve. We know the layout, access, entrance, parking, getaway. There's little traffic, it's still dinner time. All the punters cruise later. The tunnel is empty. The bus stop by the little house, the one that kept Astrid awake with the noise, is empty too. I park, switch off the motor leaving the side lights on. We march straight down the steps between the hedges and along behind the house. All the shutters are closed. The front door is locked. Big Pete takes out the knife. We look at each other then at the closed door. He nods. Then he kicks it open.

A dog barks inside. We go in and I know the interior instantaneously like the back of my hand from Astrid's diagrams, photos and Maria's description after the last time. Pete points to the jacket draped over the back of a chair. Mine. Two plastic bags sit on the table. Then a big dog comes up, tail wagging, glad to see us. Excitement! More fun than these junkies that just sit around I think he thinks. He puts his paws up on Big Pete and tries to lick him. This is one of the fierce dogs Astrid warned us about, Jazz or Strega? On the wall in large, black spray painted letters is written GOD WILL NEVER FORGIVE YOU, I BEAT WOMEN and BASTARD. He hasn't even tried to clean off her graffiti.

There's a soft voice from the stairwell, the spiral staircase he'd dragged her down.

"*Qui é*?"

"Astrid! Astrid! Get down here right away." I yell out.

"She's not here. She's at the bar" comes the reply, louder now.

Suddenly he's at the bottom of the stairs dressed in a white robe, a month old beard and his lips are drawn back grimacing showing his white teeth. His long black hair is loose and waving. He's grown a beard I notice. He's brandishing a big stick and screaming. Big Pete advances holding out the biggest blade the man has ever seen. The guy is back up the stairs quick as a cat.

Pete goes up first. All my senses are switched off. At the top, there is Astrid, dressed I notice.

"No! No!" She isn't shouting. She's crying.

"Get down those stairs! Get going!" I growl loudly but firmly and jostle her towards the stairwell.

Kazim's disappeared. He's jumped right out of the window! In the lower room I pick up my jacket from the back of the chair. I'm not going to leave that behind. A car's pulling in right outside the open doors, an astonished couple parking and the man glows in their lights. He's waving his stick and shouting for the police. We couldn't have done this more publicly if we'd advertised it beforehand. Pete puts his big arm around Astrid's neck and her body bends to his as he leads her around the back of the house, up the steps and along to the car. I run around, get in, open the passenger door and shout for them both to get in the front. Kazim is in the middle of the street screaming, beating the road with his stick, lit up by headlights of oncoming cars. Our motor starts like a bird and I take the second gap in the traffic build up. About a hundred people must have seen that little number. Made their evening!

We pass through the first arch and I suggest that maybe it would be more comfortable for Astrid if she sits on Pete's lap instead of the other way around and they swap. Everyone lights up cigarettes and I turn on Roddy Stewart again.

It's an easy getaway, easier than the last time and in minutes we're on the highway and belting back towards the lake. Not the same as last time though.

Different atmosphere. Astrid chain smokes and only speaks once. Well she shouts:

"Look Martin! See what I'm wearing?"

"I'm driving." I keep my eyes on the road but she's showing me the incriminating T-shirt she'd left behind a month ago. Fuck her I think. I only want the music.

"The first cut is the deepest".

In no time, we're off the main highway and winding through the olive groves that skirt the lake. This is where Hannibal defeated the Roman army two thousand two hundred and twelve years earlier. Across the plain, round the town and up into the hills. I have no idea what the next move is except to get home. I don't park on the piazza but pull across the tatty lawn outside the loggia. The lights are swinging in the wind. Pete virtually carries Astrid to the door. I didn't know then that she's left the boots (she said she loved) behind in the little red madhouse.

She sits on the sofa with her head in her hands and I pour three glasses of wine. One to her. I give Pete the knife. Payment for the second job. Given to me on my fiftieth birthday by a man known as Mr Garlic, oil and pepperoncino. Easy come, easy go.

Then Astrid starts:

"You really fucked it! That's it! We're finished! He saw you. He saw the car. Now we're all fucked!"

"Those dogs were a joke" says Pete. "This one comes up to me and licks my hand. About as good as a chocolate fire guard! I'm off home." and he gets up and goes over and pulls a ring off Astrid's finger, the one Maria gave her a month ago, picks up his new knife and says goodnight. Just me and Astrid left to fight it out. I let her get on with it.

"The bastard. So he gets another new knife. You betrayed me. Now I've got no one! No one! How did you dream that up? How many glasses of wine did you have to decide to do such a fucked up stunt as that? You're an alcoholic! Oh! You'll be alright with your lawyers but I'm going to prison."

"Call your father." is all I could think of saying. And she does. I don't hear what they said but when she comes back into the dining room she says her flight is in two or three days. Too late I think. Then she starts again:

"I trusted you and you broke that trust. How do you think I feel? Happy to be rescued? Glad to be safe? Did you think you were a couple of heroes come to save me? Fuck it! All the cleaning I did here. Shit!"

I don't want to mention all the cleaning, cooking, nursing, shopping and helping I've done so I don't.

"Fuck you! It was all going so well. Kaz and I made our peace. He said he understood why I did what I did. He hasn't made an official denouncement to the police. He won't trust me any more. Now he'll go to the cops for sure. I wasn't going back to get back together with him. Now I'm an arsehole. He knows I've been with you."

Good! I think. If something good comes out of this, I'll have nailed up the lid on the coffin of that relationship.

I tell her I'm not frightened. Maybe it had been a mistake. But I don't really believe that.

"He saw you! He saw the car! He was in the bushes

outside the house when we got in the car. Up until tonight, we were safe. Now he's seen everything, everyone. You really fucked up. Fuck you!"

"No he wasn't in the bushes. He was screaming and banging his stick on the road in front of the oncoming cars."

"Oh, so I was hallucinating?"

Yes, I think, just like you hallucinated that time when I came to check you out in October. You thought he was watching us when Rosemary was sitting with him in the bar all the time we were talking on the cathedral steps.

"I'm going to jail! Don't you understand? Fuck it! I'm going to jail for attempted murder. Don't you fucking understand how serious this is? Fuck it! Fuck you!"

I try to reassure her that she isn't but I feel exhausted. All last month's energy wasted. All the work we've done together is gone. We're washed up, wrung out. But she still has some fire left and she hurls it:

"So I go back to the States to what? To what? My fucked up parents? My mother? My fucked up mother who lied to me? You've just bought my ticket! Thanks a lot! Fuck it! Fuck you! I'm going to bed." She gathers up her covers and goes down to her room. Once again, her stove isn't lit.

I don't think I've ever felt worse, and then I remember the times I have, much worse. I make up my bed on the couch and try to sleep. Forget it! Up and have a cigarette. Give it another try. No good. I can't sleep. I spend two restless hours thinking what the next move could, should be and then, around three, I decide to call her father. I make sure Astrid's asleep first, calling her name outside the door of her bedroom. She's out of it.

"Hello Jim. Listen, Astrid should leave tomorrow."

He asks why.

"She went back to Kazim in Perugia and I got her out of there last night. She spent the night before with him and she lied to me saying she wouldn't see him and would stay with a girlfriend. I called her friend who said she'd seen Astrid with him. She's furious with me and doesn't trust me any more. She can't stay here any longer."

He starts on about the schedule. The next flight out is in two or three days.

"Listen Jim. Astrid has to leave tomorrow. TOMORROW."

"Isn't there someone who could stay with her till Thursday?"

"No! She's got to go IMMEDIATELY."

He gets the message at last and says he will call me back in fifteen minutes. I put on a pot of coffee. As it gargles to ready, he calls back.

"She's on tomorrow's flight. Today's for you. United. It leaves Milan at 11am. You'll have to leave at five to make it. You have to be there by nine. Here's the code number you quote at United desk. There'll be some extra to pay on her ticket but I'll reimburse you."

I write down the details and say I'll call him when she's through passport control.

"Thank you SIR!" he says and hangs up.

I collect Astrid's belongings scattered around the house and take them down to her room, turning on the light. She's asleep. Her mouth is open. She looks dead. I check she's breathing like an anxious parent. I pull her bag from under the table and start to pile her stuff up. She needs an hour minimum to get up in the morning and we leave at five, latest. Give her another ten minutes. Have coffee and get changed, ready so I can concentrate on her.

At four I wake her. She stirs and I guess what's happened hits her and she buries her head under the covers.

"Astrid. Get up. You're leaving in an hour and you've got to pack."

There's a muffled "Fuck you."

I touch her shoulder as I've often done to wake her.

"Don't touch me!" she spits. She's awake.

"I'm going to pack your things. Please get up NOW." I stuff things in her bag. She stirs again and buries herself deeper under the covers. I go upstairs leaving her alone to get out of bed. When I go down again, she's sitting on the edge of the bed she fell out of before I wedged it up. Her head's in her hands.

"Fuck you. You're sending me back to prison. Fuck you!"

"Please start packing right away."

She gets up and pulls out what I've just put in her bag. She's better with clothes than I am. Woman's touch. I leave her again for a few minutes and when I get back she's done. I carry the big bag up to the dining room and she follows with the smaller things.

I give her a glass of juice and she lights a cigarette and starts crying.

"I'm going back to prison. Fuck it! Fuck you!"

I go back down to her room and hunt around for odds and ends. A necklace, a photograph, a sock. She doesn't want any of the clothes I gave her. She's left them on the table and floor. OK. I understand. Upstairs again, she's packing properly and says there are things in the drawers downstairs which I go down and fetch. She's quiet now, resigned I hope. Getting on with the job. She packs one penny whistle.

"Where are the others?"

"I've lost them."

"Which ones do you need?"

"B flat, C and E flat." so I give her mine.

"Can I take the book?"

"Sure." That's just what she needs to read going back to the States, "The Lost Continent" by Bill Bryson, but she asks for it.

How long do we have? Ten minutes, no more. It's going to be a tight run thing as it is. She goes to the bathroom and breaks her ablution record by miles. Five o'clock. I put her bags in the car. She puts on her black leather jacket and her old, thin shoes. No new boots any more. That's what happens when you do predictably unpredictable things. She throws one last look around the room that was her home and she goes and gets in the car as I lock up the house.

Into town first to get cash. I leave her in the car outside the bank. She could drive off now and she'd have all her stuff with her and wheels. Back to Perugia?

She drove the car before I did. How much cash to take out? 400 thou'?

We're off down the one way hill the wrong way to the lower town for diesel. Self Service. The pump is fifty metres from the cash desk. Another chance for her to make a break. Shit I'm exhausted and we've hardly left. How am I going to get through this one? I put in enough to get to the first service station along the Autostrada.

I'm going to try the trains first. Arezzo station. Roads are clear but I know there's going to be ice and fog to come and a rush hour outside Milan. We race along the night road. If only it was this empty going to school and back. I pull into the station but the trains are no good. We wouldn't make it. Going to have to drive it and it's off to the Autostrada. Fast. At the toll gate I take off my jacket. Astrid's got the heating on full blast and she's smoked three cigarettes already. Heavy goods vehicles on the road but fast moving. We're racing. Tyres not too good but it's dry, thank God. We're the fastest on the road, leaving everything standing. I leave the lights on full. Over the Arno and down into the valley. Even faster now, 155, 160. There's still another 20 ks under there. Mist thickening but I can't let up.

We pull in at the service station.

"Breakfast time."

"Good." says Astrid. That's progress I think. In the bar she orders a pannino and a beer. Small or medium asks the bar man? Large says Astrid. Medium I correct. I have a sandwich and a cappucino and finish it while she's not half way through hers.

"Can you wait here while I go and fill up the car please?"

The pump is two hundred metres from the bar and there's a big jeep having a full service. Astrid's got another chance to bolt. By the time the jeep's through and my car's half full, Astrid walks over with the remains of her pannino and gets in. Another good sign. She's going along with it now. I ask the attendant how many hours to Milan? Three and a half. Heavy fog in the Valpadana. Another forty minutes from the autostrada to the airport. Back on the road I tell Astrid it's going to be touch and go and wonder how we're going to spend the next twenty four hours if we don't make it.

"Can I put some music on please?" Sure. Rod Stewart again. The Best of Roddy.

"I am sailing, I am sailing....."

Within minutes, she's asleep with her mouth open. She'll start snoring soon I know so I turn up the music. Firenze sud, Certosa, traffic thick but no trucks allowed in the fast lane. 165 klms per hour. Firenze nord, Calenzaro, then we're climbing into the Appenines. Snow on surrounding hills but the road is ice-free from the traffic. Signs overhead give -3° C and tell me to drive prudently. If only you knew, message!

Tunnels and trucks but as my headlights grow quickly in their wing mirrors, they're letting me pass. Over the summit then down to Bologna. Astrid was here just over a month ago, sleeping in cardboard boxes, trading her white-gold birthday bracelet for a pair of leg warmers before going back and getting fucked by the Turk.

Onto the plain now and here's the light of the dawn. Beautiful church on the hill. Then we hit the fog. Can't slow down. Big cars coming up behind. Faster than the Golf. I push it to 175 kph but the wheels start to vibrate. OK. That's my max. Pull over and let them pass, then out into the fast lane again. If in doubt, accelerate. I learnt that when I was a kid. We soar past the juggernauts with visibility next to zilch. I cannot die now, we cannot die on this trip. I cannot let my daughter hear that I died, crashed, doing this insane stunt. Astrid has to get there alive even if she dies afterwards. I don't want to die with her. She said the other night: Death - piece of cake. Life - piece of shit. I'm not going to die but I'm so tired.

The fog's thinning then thickening again. She's still asleep. Switch to The Grateful Dead. Astrid music. She was never the same after Jerry Garcia died in the summer. Took it personally. Modena, Parma, Piacenza. Coming up to half past eight. Traffic's thickening, and the fog. Signs say a foggy right to Milan. It clears in the city with urban updraft I guess. Lodi. I've got to watch for exit signs but we go through the toll gate first. Nine. Nine ten. Toll-gate 1000 metres. Choose the shortest queue, the one with two trucks not six cars. 30.500 Lire. Jesus! I hope I brought enough money. There's always the bank card. Bang goes my Christmas money. I wanted to take my daughter and Astrid to Ravenna. I wonder what it would have been like if they'd met. They've spoken on the phone a couple of times. So different. I'm so lucky to have such an easy daughter. This one's making up for it. I wonder if she thinks of me as her kidnapper? She's already been kidnapped once. Astrid. Asteroid. Wild Flower. Endangered Species. Switch back to Rod Stewart.

"I can tell by your eyes that you've probably been crying for ever."

Here's the exit to Malpensa. Traffic's thick. Late rush hour. Astrid wakes up. She's slept three hours. I wonder what her first thoughts are. She's silent, smoking and tries the Dylan tape but the machine won't accept it so it's back to Roddie.

"The first cut is the deepest..."

Traffic thickens, slows then we stop. Crawl. Stop. Crawl. Big exit to Monza and Como. Then it clears again and we're off. I'm quickly up to 150 and remember I'm in the city and slow down to 120. Half nine. We're half an hour late already but the flight leaves at eleven so we have time to make it, just.

We're heading into the country. Sometimes the airport is signed, sometimes not. If I miss the turn or take a wrong one? Can't happen. Only on the way back. Shall I have a sleep once she's through and out? I'm not as tired as I was an hour ago.

There's the turn off to the airport. We're going to make it - alive. Towers of the airport and a plane taking off. Turn into the airport and slow down behind a short queue of cars.

Fuck! A police block. Polizia. Two cars and three machine guns. They're letting all the cars through. We get to the slowing ramp and a policeman waves me over to the side. Jesus, right at the doorstep they get us. The car's been checked over a few times and so far has got through each time. But now?

"Astrid, get your passport ready."

I get out and pull out my wallet for my licence slowly, so the machine gun pointing at me doesn't think I'm drawing a weapon.

"Documents of the car and the signorina's passport." He knows she's a miss. I hand them over and he walks over to his car. He's on to his radio. A catwalk beautiful police woman guards me.

"Where's she going?" she asks. A beautiful woman in a military uniform carrying a machine gun. I can see why Castro and Gadaffi go for them. She knows Astrid's going, not me.

"To America."

"Is it cold in America too now?"

"Not where she's going, California. It hardly ever gets cold there."

The policeman is writing down the details of the documents. He speaks again into his phone then he walks back over towards us. This is it. He hands me the pink licence, the little blue/black passport and the white log book and he's telling me to go. I can't believe it! I give Astrid her passport and drive to international departures, drop her off with her bag. I'm going to park the car. I'll meet her at the United desk.

I have to go right around again and through the block which the police are dismantling. Job done? I ask where I can park and they say down there on your right. Dropped off my passenger on her own. They can see.

Into the pay park and leave the car in a handicapped space. Otherwise there's no room at the inn.

I walk over to departures and find Astrid at the United desk. The uniformed lady explains that her ticket has expired. I smile, pleading. She's got to get on that flight. I've got 250.00 Lire cash. Don't mention my bank card. She goes off to check with someone somewhere. God? We wait. I've left my cigarettes in the car. Take one of Astrid's. She's silent. Resigned? The lady comes back and smiles. $150. That's 240.000 lire. I pay up and she says she hasn't got change but she's making Astrid's ticket valid. I go to find change but no one's got any. I go back and the lady's left her desk. Astrid's waiting at check in. Her shoulders are stooped and her jeans baggy. I ask her for money to make up the 40.00 Lire. No, only 2.000. She's offered me ten. My money. Remains of her last allowance.

She says that maybe this is all for the best. One of the things I have tried to teach her is that everything happens for the best because it happens, although that philosophy is shot with holes. I explain my fears for myself on my journey back and then say that it's my problem thinking about her journey back. I'm going home. She's leaving home.

I pay the lady at the United desk and wait for Astrid to check in. A man with an ID card is talking to her. He says something and makes her laugh. Good. Then she's done. 10.50. I walk her over to passport control wondering what to say. At the gate I turn and we give each other a weak hug and I say Good Luck. She says Thanks then she's through.

I wait, watching the policeman in his glass box as

Astrid gets close. Last hurdle. Her visa's more than three months expired. They can't stop her now. She's at the window. Then she's through.

Relax at last.

She turns to look back.

Don't look back Astrid.

She's gone.

12

The Flying Squad

I can't sleep now. I'm wide awake. If I sleep, I'll sleep for ever. My brother told me the secret of long drives when you're tired: stop and snack often. So, let's get to the first stop. Back on to the ring road. The sun's shining and I'm relying on my pal Rod to get me home.

"You're in my heart, you're in my soul, you're my lover, my best friend...."

I miss the first service station. Nearly hit a truck. Next one can't be far. Astrid must be boarding now. Pull in at the the Agip sign. Cappucino and sandwich. Pee. Cigarettes. Then take the car to fill up. Smart attendant points out blobs of diesel on the fifth door. Check your air filter? He gives me no choice. It's filthy and he walks off with a limp haddock in his hand and returns with a new one and fits it. Check the oil? I guess. A kilo. Can I pay with my card? Cash running low. Had to pay a lot extra for a ticket at the airport. Pull over, park, go into the office and tap in the code.

All set and off. Try to keep my speed reasonable as traffic is heavy, then suddenly I'm lost! I'm driving into the centre of Milan. Shoot! Stop and ask the way. Pretend I'm Swiss and get good directions. Keep going, straight. Half an hour later I hit the circular road and then onto the Sole Mio. The car enjoys its filter and oil and travels better, faster though it still vibrates over 170. Of course it's lighter without its passenger and baggage. Her heaviest baggage weighed nothing. Then I realise that if I slow down to 130, I'm less tense, it's less tiring and I tuck in behind a black Mercedes from Rome. Lady driver so don't go to close. I've heard of Italian drivers trying to pick up single ladies on the road. She's going to be my pacer. Don't count the K's. Just check the mirror regularly.

Astrid's gone now. Mustn't think about her. Stay alive.

Piacenza, Parma, Modena. No, don't go to Venice! It would be fun though. I promised to take Astrid there at Carnival. We planned to play penny whistles in the *cali,* wearing masks.

Before I know it I'm past Bologna and climbing into the mountains. The Merc from Rome doesn't seem to mind pacing me. It's helped. Heavy traffic's all going the other way. Maybe I should get off at Florence and go to my friends and ask if I can stop over the night but then all those explanations.

Tunnels, viaducts. A Ducato turbo van gives me a hard time. Got better cornering than I have. Merc still in front. One slip and I would smash into the central barrier. Kidnapper dies on Autosole! Instantaneous. No one knows where I am. Maybe I should stop and call the lady on the hill? But that would only frighten her.

"Tonight's the night. Gonna be alright." Roddy keeps me on track.

Firenze nord. Two police cars taking up the outside lane and going too slowly. Other cars overtake. I've lost the Merc. Pass the cops. Fuck it. Swiss tourist. Signa, Certosa, tunnels, Firenze sud. Stop for another cappucino and sandwich on the other side of the road from where Astrid and I had breakfast nine hours earlier. Big beer she ordered! She could drink me under the table. Accused me of being an alcoholic and I said I only tried to keep up with her.

Home stretch. No traffic to speak of and I go up to pre-wheel-vibration speed. Arezzo! Home! I made it! Now don't go and blow it. Go to the station and get a paper. I'll do the crossword at home. Keep my mind on simple problems.

"Carry me to my own folks. That's where I want to be."

Back on the commuting route from school to home. Know every inch and bump. Pass heavy police block below the town. Four cars and at least fifteen men, armed. Both sides of the road. I'm tucked behind a builder's van going home after work. Sneak through. Then up the hill, past the cemetery, round the Etruscan wall and up into the mountains.

Beautiful red sunset. Great ball of fire. Shepherd's delight. Over the top, through the pass and cruise along the high flat. Three bends to go. Astrid's corner the second last. How long will it stay her corner? Probably for ever. Over the bridge, straight, then our big oak trees and pull up. Check the mail. Christmas cards and electricity bill. Then down the drive and home. I'm alive! Astrid's alive! Safe! And I'm home.

The stove's still in after twenty hours and I pull out the air baffle and roar it up. The cats are arching their backs for their supper. Got a fax to send first.

"Jim. Astrid got on the flight. Call me."

Feed the cats. A friend calls from Scotland, wondering what's going on. Must have sent a wrong signal. She says she's glad she called.

I call Patrizia, the woman doctor who was to examine Astrid this evening for the second time. I tell her she's gone, sorry. She went back to the guy who did the damage you were going to check out. She says she's sorry for Astrid. I agree. Aren't we all. Isn't Astrid?

Her father calls. What sort of mood was she in? Angry at first, then quiet. Resigned. Tired and in shock. Needs rest and a doctor. Please call me or fax me when she's arrived. Thanks both ways.

Call a friend who needs to know. She asks if I'm OK. I didn't die did I? My sister comes down and I give her a brief rundown. Then have a baked potato and grilled sausage. It's been sandwiches for twenty four hours. Glass of wine. Another, then it's into my notes and change some of those names. Done. Pete and Maria are safe unless they torture me. Then I write another fax to Astrid's father.

"I don't want any money. She's an ENDANGERED SPECIES. Take care of her." Go to the table to pour another glass and there are two large white cars pulling up outside the house. Black leather coats coming across the lawn and suddenly the house is full of men. Policemen!

"Maaartin?" A badge is flashed.

"Yes. Entrate."

They fill the room, each door covered. Definitely not a hit squad. Two go and search the house. The tallest who has a hard, gentle face asks me where I was last night. No hesitation.

"Taking a young girl from a dangerous situation."

"Where is she now?"

"On a flight to the States."

"Flight number?"

"Here, it's written on my board by the phone." He copies it down. The phone rings. It's my sister asking if I'm alright? She's seen the cars with their plates from Perugia.

"Yes, I'm fine. Just very tired."

"Where's she gone?" says bulging black leather.

"To her father's."

"Were you paid to do it?"

"Look, here's a fax I just sent him." I translate. Then it's copied on the fax machine. A shorter one presses buttons I never knew existed and the fax machine prints out the last days faxes. Numbers match. Then there are phones ringing in pockets and mine rings again but all the calls are for them. He's co-operating I hear them call through. Everyone relaxes.

I tell them I did it for her own good. He drugged her, raped her and beat her. He tried to make her hook for him and nearly sold her. He's a heroin addict. She was like another daughter to me, more than just my best student. She was here a month recovering and then she went back. I decided she was in danger and took her out.

"Who helped you this time and the last time you visited this guy?"

"I can't say until I've spoken to my lawyer."

"What nationality is he?"

"I can't say. Listen, I'll give you written notes of all the things that he did to her."

They crowd round my desk as the little printer spits it all out. Names changed just in time. I think they trust me now. I feel safe with them. I like having them around. They're a cool bunch of guys as my daughter would say. They like the warmth from the stove.

"It's even got his name on it. Look! Nice stereo. Pretty terracotta heads. Where did you get those? In the antique market in Arezzo?" They're going through the stolen goods.

"Who's painting is that?"

"Mine. No. I didn't paint it. It was given to me, like the stereo."

"Who is it by?"

"There's his signature."

Another phone call comes through and there's a quick chatter.

"Now you have to come with us."

"To Perugia? OK, as long as I can smoke and sleep in the car."

I shut up the house and we're off.

I'm faster on the mountain road than they are but then I drive it five hundred times a year and have been for the last twenty years. Nearly ten thousand times more than them. I tell them I have a button called *casa* installed in each car and I only have to press it and the car takes me home. Once I've shown them a short cut below the town and we're on the plain, they take off. They ask if I like Perugia but I like Siena the best. I don't tell them that I hate the city we're approaching. We discuss the difference between Tuscans and Umbrians. It all boils down to earthquakes. In Umbria, earthquakes force people to co-operate. Who knows when you'll need your friends to dig you out of the rubble?

They teach me a new way into Perugia if I can remember it, if I need it. The number of times I've got lost here, ending up in strange parts. The car park outside the police station is full so they have to squeeze in and I'm taken upstairs and shown some armchairs at the end of a corridor and all I can think about is sleep. I'm woken by "Maartin. *Vieni.*" I go into a room where a man is at a computer.

"What is the name of your lawyer?" I tell them. They let me go back to my chair.

I'm woken up by my lawyer. How did he get here? It's past one. We go and sit in another room and I give him a brief description of events and he asks for the name of my friend. I ask what will happen to him.

"The sooner you give it, we get his statement and we clear this all up."

I ask my friends to leave us alone and then I tell the lawyer about big Pete and where he lives. I feel sick now. Sick and tired. I remember writing to my daughter saying Astrid was trouble with a capital T. Why didn't I take my own advice?

The lawyer and I make a statement to the man in front of the computer and we both sign it. We make another, denouncing Astrid's lover, all he did to her. My friend adds the printouts I gave him and the copies of the faxes saying I gave them willingly. Then we're done. I notice there's an accusation from Kazim lying there. He lied to Astrid or she lied to me. Probably both.

It's past three. I've had an hour's sleep in forty hours and driven and been driven over a thousand kilometres. Now they're going to take me home. I shake hands with those staying behind and get in the back of the white Alfa. I learn a new exit from the city and we're down and out, past the hookers getting out of punters' cars or waiting for the last ones to pick them up. This is where I could have found Astrid in another few weeks if she'd stayed on, but she's out of it.

On the way home, the driver says we did a good job. Morally right, but the law is the law. They want to see where Pete lives. When we arrive in the lower town I show them, and I ask that when they go to get him I can be there to talk to him first. They agree and they'll come for me tomorrow morning after ten.

"Pete might be at work."

"What does he do?" I tell them, leaving out the how-to-kill bit.

At home, they go through the car documents again asking about the name in the log book. I don't lie. I'm too exhausted to lie. But they stop short of telling me I'm driving a stolen car. It's after four and I just want to lie down. They say goodnight and go home or back to work.

13

Hangover

I got up at seven. Big Pete. Should I warn him? No. Yes! Quickly! Hide the knife. No! No! Trust them. They trusted me.

I went to town to have coffee and buy cigarettes and got home for ten. Half-ten, they called me to meet them in the square near Big Pete's place.

It was market day and the place was packed so I parked alongside the main road and waited. Four hours sleep in forty eight and I was high. It's like a dream, being in an aquarium with all those exotic fish swimming by. The Swiss girl who knitted the pullover I was wearing came up and told me twice she was going shopping. Did I look that bad? She commented on the car's plates.

My friends were late. A Vigili approached and I said I'm waiting for the police but he didn't want to know. My first computer teacher buzzed past on his motorino waving. The street was crowded. Men in hats were doing weekly deals. A girl put a flyer under my windscreen wiper and I scrumpled it up and lit yet another cigarette. They were half an hour late and they drive fast. They can't have missed the car and gone in for Pete without me could they?

"Maartin."

There they were. They turned at the lights and pulled up behind me and we shook hands. I was glad to see them smiling. They looked glad to see me. I drove in front and led them round to near Pete's place, parked in a rare space on market day and got in behind them and directed them to Pete's door. They parked right outside in the only space left. He was out. They wrote down his and Maria's names and asked questions about her.

"Did she come on the first job? Why did she go back to England? How long have I known them? Where does Pete work? Who with?"

We waited an hour. Then I made a suggestion.

"He's at lunch with his workmates and I promise I don't know where. Let me go home, eat, sleep and let's meet at five when the market's finished. He'll be home at six at the latest."

They agreed and took me back to my car.

A wonderful spaghetti *al carbonara* and three hours sleep later, I was a new person. I went down to meet them. There was still a market as it was the last few days before Christmas, but it was quieter and warmer with coloured lights and children playing football.

"Pete's not back."

"Did you warn him?"

"No. Absolutely. You must trust me the way I trust you. I've never lied to you and I've co-operated all the way down the line. Let's go for a walk around the market. He's bound to be back soon."

We went window and stall shopping, me and a plainclothes policeman on either side. It felt safe. I met Patrizia, the doctor who was to give Astrid her second examination the evening before. She looked at my two bodyguards and smiled. Later I told them who she was. We chatted about Africa and why I came to live in Italy. Then it was back to big Pete's to wait in the dark.

Just before six his landlady arrived and I asked her for the location of the gym where Pete worked and as her son started to explain, under the street lamp up walked Big Pete.

"OK Pete. Don't worry and please trust me. Please. The police are here and I trust them. They know everything and I only gave them your name after I'd seen my lawyer. They're on our side. They think we did a good job but they want to clear everything up."

He looked angry. His eyes were small. Then he grinned and said "Fine."

I introduced him to my friends and they shook hands. Pete unlocked the door, went in and threw his jacket over the Gurkha knife lying on the sofa. They asked if he'd come to Perugia with them and he said sure. Did he want to change? No. Get his coat? No. He didn't feel the cold and anyway the coat was doing a cover up job.

We got in the back of the white Alfa and off we

went, I hoped for the last time for a long time to the place that made me sick to think about it.

I explained to the two officers that I wanted to tell Pete in English what had happened during the last twenty four hours and I'd give them an interpretation at every stage. The driver said they trusted me and then they were onto the radio calling up their interpreter to be ready when we got there. I gave Pete the run down, repeated it in Italian and then there was silence for the rest of the journey except for the radio phone occasionally cutting in, and their answers.

As we climbed into the city, the driver asked me if I knew anyone else in Perugia?

"Yes. A lady who used to work at the same school in Arezzo where Astrid went. Her name is Rosemary."

"Rosmary Talenti?" he asked.

"Yes!" How does she fit in here?

He laughed.

"How did you find me?" I asked.

"That's top secret" the driver laughed.

"We looked your name up in the phone book." said his mate.

I wanted to ask how they found my name in the first place but didn't, then I thought - Rosemary. She must have. But so soon?

I led Pete into the police station and up the stairs. I felt at home. He probably did too. We sat in the armchairs and an elderly man introduced himself as Pete's lawyer. I went over my version and when I got to the kidnapping, we were joined by one of my leather jacketed friends and a young, dark, good looking man dressed in a yellow suit. He listened attentively to the end of the story and then Pete was taken off for interrogation.

The young man introduced himself and invited me into his office. He was the head of the Flying Squad. He apologised for not being there last night but they were very busy. He offered me an armchair and sat across the table. I asked if I could smoke and he lit up too.

He asked how it all began and I started back at the school and my clever young pupil called Astrid. I went through the whole story. He listened attentively. I told him some of the other students' backgrounds just to put Astrid's into a broader perspective. He winced. Then he told me why they couldn't just throw Kazim out of the country.

"He's a political refugee. Even if he is a heroin addict. We might prosecute him for what he did and tried to do with the girl but we'd prefer to accept mutual dropping of accusations. Some of the things that go on in this city make Kazim seem like a jewel. For every woman you see standing on the side of the road, there are four Albanians living off her." He made two little exclamation mark signs with his fingers.

"But why, with Siena, a university town, don't the same problems exist?" I asked.

"Size of the city" he said. "This city is bad and I come from Naples. I haven't been able to see my parents for two months and they only live 150 kilometres away."

We talked on for an hour or more and finally, he looked me in the eye and said:

"I don't understand why you didn't come to us in the first place?"

"It honestly never occurred to me." I replied honestly.

He showed me the local newspaper for the day. There was a photo of Kazim with a woollen hat and a young beard to hide his scar, peering out of his doorway on the front page. "They took my fiancée away from me." he was quoted as saying. "I live in fear for my life." Good! You rat!

The gentleman in the yellow suit apologised for the press coverage and explained that there had been two other cases of women being been beaten in the last two days. Astrid being American, this story beat them. They'd been onto the American Embassy and they're getting in touch with her father. Relax.

He went to see how things were going with Big Pete and came back saying they were nearly through. He had to go now but I could make myself at home until they were done and if ever I needed his help I shouldn't hesitate to call him. We shook hands and I said goodbye to one of the most charming, intelligent and efficient young Italian men I have ever met. No more police jokes ever, I promised to myself.

I sat and looked through a beautifully produced book on Naples until a man came in and asked me to sit outside as he wanted to close the office for the night.

Big Pete was through by nine and afterwards the lawyer offered me his card in case I needed someone to defend me in court. We all shook hands and got back into one of the fast white cars, jumped all the red lights through town and were on to the highway in minutes. The last getaway? The driver said it was a bad thing the knife job, but otherwise everything we did, we did well. Very well.

It took us even less time for them to take us back to Pete's and we hardly had a minute to talk about our favourite holiday islands when we'd arrived. The driver had had almost as little sleep as I during the last two days and nights and less to eat and he wanted to get home. They dropped us off and he gave me his phone number and asked, not told me, to call him when I heard of Astrid's safe arrival. He said they'd call by and visit me when they were next in the area.

Pete and I went up to town and had two large glasses of draught Guinness, the best I have ever tasted, and the finest pizzas in the world and he treated me. I drove him back and went home where there was a message on the answering machine saying Astrid arrived safely. I called her dad.

"Yes, she's OK. Jet lagged obviously. She thinks she's pregnant. She's going to see doctors soon. I believe you did the right thing. And thank you." She'd lied to me again.

I called up the Flying Squad to tell them she was back with her father then had a few glasses of wine to celebrate. I put Mozart's clarinet concerto on the new stereo and turned up the volume so loud the two little speakers Pete had wired up to Astrid's powerful amplifier (that she'd ripped out of the little red madhouse) blew out.

Then the newspapers began. I'd seen the first article in the local paper on the desk of the Director of the Flying Squad but thought it would stop there. The next morning in town, sitting in the Café des Artistes, reading the comics in the 'erald and the news in the better Italian paper, it didn't cross my mind to look for any notice of recent activities in this part of the world. I paid my bill and, just before leaving, took a peek at the local paper, out of habit, not fear, see the new statistics for the last tourist season or read about some new Etruscan discovery.

Instead, front page headlines!

TEACHER KIDNAPS HIS PUPIL ON HER FATHER'S ORDERS!

Fuck! Get out of town quick. In the street outside I met some friends just back from the States.

"Help! I've just seen the papers. Please come and read an article to me. I can't. I'll be sick."

They read it and reassured me all accusations were in inverted commas. "Kidnapped". "Fiancée". They bought me a strong drink and went on reading: "Englishman.... Art history teacher.... Fiftyish..... Golf with Swiss plates.... Arezzo..."

I politely asked about their lives but didn't hear what they said. I needed to go home. The paper printed everything except my name. I thanked them and left.

Outside the newsagents there was a poster. It usually shouted the lead story. "Gold factory robbed of 100 millions worth." " Family of four mushroom hunters struck by lightening." "Hunter shoots himself in the foot."

Kidnapped
on the orders of her
Daddy. She wanted to
run away for the love
of her young 'undesirable'.

Young? He's twice her age. I was old at his age. Had to get out of Dodge fast, had to go home.

No, I had to hide out somewhere close but a secret. My Irish friend Bernadetta lives about five kilometres away with her Italian partner, their young daughter and a bun in her oven. I called her when I got home and asked if I could take refuge at her house and hide my car for a few days. She was game so I threw some things into the Golf and drove down the dirt road to the bottom of the valley, shut my car away in her garage and hibernated in her guest room.

The night before Christmas Eve, we were all invited to a party but there would be people there who were my friends once, but think that they're not any longer and to have to make polite conversation with them when every pause would bring Astrid and the recent nightmare back into painfully sharp focus, no, it was beyond me. 'Detta understood and I wished them a pleasant evening but they had their own problems with the new baby due.

When they'd left, I drove off home in the little Renault that I was using as a lifeboat. I revved the engine so hard to get up their muddy road in the mist and rain that the fan belt snapped.

Along the main road close to home there was a car in front of me, driving slowly in the mist and it turned down the drive to my house. Not a sharp journalist I prayed.

It was Big Pete! I knew it was the right thing not going to the party. We pulled up together and my big buddy, my dependable friend, wiped his boots, went inside and took off his jacket throwing it over the back of a chair, feeling more at home than I did though I was safer with him there. He was body guarding me again. He wanted a game of dommies but I wasn't really up to it. I'd some calls to make and afterwards, we sat and chatted about the last few days.

I told him I was lying low but came back to hide a piece of paper which had Astrid's handwriting on it and I found it on my desk under the last two faxes to her father. I read it to him:

Everything Kazim did to me (that I remember)

1. *Beat my ribs with a bamboo stick.*
2. *From behind my back he punched me with his fist on the bridge of my nose, leaving me with two weeks worth of black eyes.*
3. *He bent my fingers backwards to the extent that I had to move my hand in order for my fingers not to break." (She said she couldn't play the penny whistles for days afterwards)*
4. *Slaps in the face.*
5. *He threw me on the ground, I don't exactly know how.*
6. *He pulled me down the stairs by my hair bruising my head and ankles.*
7. *He left bruises in the shape of fingerprints on my arms and neck.*

8. *He picked me up by my neck so that I was gasping for air.*
9. *He bruised me on my legs.*
10. *He punched me on my mouth so my lips were swollen.*
11. *He told me God would never forgive me.*
12. *He threatened me that he would kill me and cut me with his knife.*
13. *And more than that I don't remember because I don't want to.*

I'd forgotten about the other half of the paper and Big Pete suggests I tear it off and keep the two halves separately. It was a good thing for Astrid the police didn't find this. It read:

What I think should happen to him:

1. *Everything and worse with NO mercy.*
2. *He should live in order to feel pain and always remember that pain.*
3. *He should have a scar diagonally across his face for life which should read I am a bastard.*
4. *His hair should be shaved, buzzed.*
5. *The first thing people say when they see him should be What happened to you?*
6. *He knows that I am giving him only half the pain he gave to me.*
7. *He should feel shame and embarrassment and his false sense of pride should be crushed.*
8. *The only mercy is that he should live to feel his own pain.*

9. *I give him my life, my love. I defend him and he beats me in the street, dragging me home so that he can really give it to me.*

These two parts of the same sheet of paper in Astrid's scrawly writing were my insurance policy. The first half I could use if we ever went to court to show what he did to her. The other half would help Big Pete get off the hook I hoped, if he ever got on it again.

I felt better and we had a couple of games of dommies and he beat me soundly then said goodbye and left. I started to prepare the supper (I'd precooked for Astrid when she got back from Perugia) when the phone rang:

"Martin? Hi, it's Astrid."

"Hi. How are you?"

"Oh, OK I guess. Tired. I've seen a doctor and I'm resting up. How are you?"

"Tired too. Exhausted mentally and physically."

"Hey, thanks for what you did. Maybe it was for the best in the end."

"You're welcome." I said. "Any time you need to have an abusive boyfriend beaten up and scarred for life, or you might want to be kidnapped and deported or receive one-on-one penny whistle tuition, or maybe instruction on laying gold leaf or feel the urge to get laid by someone old enough to be your father, you know where to come. As they say."

That's not really what I said but I'm glad I didn't go to that Christmas party.

14

Aftermath

After Astrid got back to San Francisco we began a virtual relationship. We faxed each other in Etruscan writing which I'd taught her so her dad couldn't read what we wrote, although, as the letters were all back to front, it wasn't difficult.

She'd moved into her dad's apartment, sleeping on a pull down bed in his living room and once a week she called me, long calls, often shutting herself in the bathroom out of her dad's earshot or lying in her fold up bed holding on to her silver ankle chain. She talked about settling in back home where there was no home.

At first her calls were tentative and nervous, enquiries about police, journalists, victims and accusations. As her confidence grew and she felt safer, she passed on news of her life and the new people she drew into her magnetic minefield. What became obvious was that she had no friends, no people of her own age with whom she had had long lasting friendships. She'd burnt her boats all the way down the line. That's how I became her best friend. She told me things about her new life that a young lady of her age would normally confide to a female peer.

These were the milestones she mentioned:

In February she turned down heroin. She signed on at the SF Academy of Art studying to be a war photographer. In March, she smoked crack with a couple of guys then let one of them fuck her without using a condom.

"That's what young people do around here" she informed me.

"Why don't you just throw away the results of your AIDS tests and take up Russian Roulette?" I reinformed her.

Nights after that she started sleeping with the barman she'd made friends with and he used a condom so everything was fine.

Her grandmother gave her the old family Cadillac which she described as "jigger, jigger, jigger and that's ten dollar's worth of gas." Crossing the Bay Bridge and stopping to pay at the toll booth she was told the two guys in the car in front had already paid her fare.

In April she told me her dad was dying. At the end of the month she called to say she'd been clean, off drugs and alcohol for nine days. She'd started heroin two weeks before, nearly sold her ass to pay for the fourth fix but passed out in a public toilet trying to find a vein after counting twenty nine holes in her body with blood everywhere.

She called up Narcotics Anonymous and began the twelve stage program, one day at a time, everyday being the first day of the rest of her life.

We'd talked about meeting up in the summer, going to Africa, maybe. Then it was Mexico, then it was nowhere. No way anywhere was all I could see. It was time to cut off. But she reminded me I was her best friend and where was a best friend when she really needed one even though she was just a voice from the other side of the planet. A voice with a new hair colour, a lip ring and another through her navel, tattoos, the works. She was hitchhiking through her young life and I was always there to give her a ride. So we agreed we would meet up in London.

We'd planned three weeks together with pre-established rules of obedience and chastity but after two days and nights we mutually decided one unforgettable week together was better than dragging it out. And it was.

The day she arrived, jet lagged and exhausted, after giving me a tour of her rings and tattoos, she got stuck butt down in a hip bath in the apartment friends had lent us. We walked on Hampstead Heath and had tea at Kenwood House before I dropped her off at her first AA/NA meeting at which she not only shared but chaired, reducing fifty alcoholics to helpless hysterical laughter.

On the way to her second meeting in Knightsbridge, we detoured through Covent Garden, Soho, Chinatown, Trafalgar Square, The Mall, St. James' Park, Marble Arch and the Serpentine. Along the way she chatted about Daisy, her Lebanese school friend from when she was thirteen, at the American School just outside London. Daisy used to live around Green Park somewhere.

We slept on either side of a large, double bed, in an apartment in Kentish Town, she with dried out camomile tea bags over her eyes and headphones on, snoring. In the street on a night time walk revisiting my past I found a little clasp with fake diamonds in the surround and an orange stone set in it and I woke her, pinning it to her night T-shirt.

We talked about drugs, drink, recovery, money, photography, my daughter, the house in Italy, Big Pete and Maria, her father's five girlfriends and the KGB, her mother's vanity and drunken car smashes, her grandma's melon farm in Napa Valley and what it was like living on the San Andreas fault line. We discussed her aim of completing goals, music, food, her interest in cooking implements and was I going to follow up the Africa lead? We talked about dreams and nightmares, farting and shitting, menstruation, her grandmother's fruit packing business hiring immigrant Mexican labourers, her men friends, lovers and her ambitions, her song lyrics and photographs, Kazim and black leather, spiritualism and St. Francis, fear and anger, love and choices, death and letting go of each other. We agreed that London was a short excursion for her, a brief crossing as she was on the far side of an ever widening river. She refused to talk about last winter, towards the end of those four weeks before I kidnapped her, as we started to have snow fights and wrestling matches on the floor. She never mentioned some of the things we discussed on the phone those next six months following her return to the US, obsessions, what started exactly a year ago, her best friend. We did teas here and there, ate Thai take away, played the penny whistle and laughed a lot. She said she wanted to lose one layer of epidermis so her actual muscles showed and she'd be like Batwoman.

She'd been the emotional centre of my life for one year and it was time to move on but she still had some cards upon which to draw. She led me to a place in Regent's Park I recognized from when I went there with my grandmother nearly fifty years earlier.

On our last day, after a late breakfast, we went to the National Gallery where I wanted to check out the slides for my forthcoming lectures. Astrid opted to go and take photos around the market at St. Martin's-in-the-Field and we met an hour later, overlooking Trafalgar Square. She was clearly jolted. She told me she'd just met Mojo, the guy who'd introduced her to Kazim back in Perugia a year ago.

There was an open-air rock concert billed to take place in Hyde Park. It was the biggest open-air concert in London since the sixties. Bob Dylan, The Who and who else but Eric Clapton. We sat in front of a hot dog stand outside the ticket-only enclosure, rhododendrons blocking any view of what I'd seen all years ago, eating french fries and drinking tea.

Eric said, VERY loudly, "Christ, I was here twenty seven years ago listening to The Rolling Stones!"

"So was I!" I wanted to scream at the top of my voice but I said it softly to Astrid who was huddled up on our park bench with ketchup smeared round her mouth.

"I was up a tree with fans dropping down from branches like autumn leaves as Mick Jagger released butterflies and recited Shelley in memory of Brian Jones who'd died the week before. That night, we saw Chuck Berry and The Who at the Albert Hall. All the black leather clad rockers came charging down the aisles in the first half followed by British bobbies and in the second half the rockers threw pennies at Roger Daltry as they reworked Tommy. I've never needed to go to a rock concert ever since."

That evening with Astrid, on our ring-side park bench like an elderly married couple listening to "Leyla", "Darling, you look wonderful tonight" and the best ever version yet of "Badge" as it echoed in quadrophonia off the Knightsbridge buildings, I couldn't resist turning to her as I wiped the snot from her sneeze off my sleeve and whispering into her ear "Darling, they're playing our music."

On our way back in the crowds, we took a side street south of Oxford Street and both, for the first time, saw Concorde flying through the night sky.

Back in our oasis, I gave her Kazim's knife I'd stolen from Big Pete who'd stolen it from her who'd stolen it from Kazim that night, long ago in Perugia. She wrapped it in newspaper and put it in the bottom of her packed bag saying she'd probably just throw it in the Pacific Ocean when she got back.

We said goodbye the next morning on the 134 bus. She was going to stay with a former user for a night and we agreed to meet at Hammersmith Underground station on Monday morning.

She was there waiting for me, blotchy and pale.

On the train to the airport she told me she'd been to this meeting the night before and afterwards, over coffee, she'd met Daisy's sister George who'd put her in touch with Daisy, (her friend from when she was thirteen) who was a drummer in a rock band back in San Francisco. I realised then that she was on her own in all of this.

At the airport check-in, she asked me to go because she didn't like goodbyes, so I kissed her, whispered a secret into her ear and walked off, never looking back.

A few weeks later back in Italy she called to tell me she'd got a job, paid off her credit card and the money she stole from her Dad, rented an apartment and got promotion. I asked her what her job was?

"A stripper" she said. "There's no physical contact with the audience and it's great money."

She'd been promoted to the desk; whatever that meant.

Some weeks later she told me she was the bass guitarist in a band and wasn't going back to stripping though she was the best there was. Her college work was going well and her drawing teacher said she was awesome. She planned to study natural medicines.

I called her on 4th November. She said she had wanted to speak to me but was worried about her phone bill. Then she pulled another rabbit from the hat:

"There's something I've wanted to tell you so I wrote you a letter but haven't mailed it yet."

"Oh, come on Astrid. We both do this to each other. Tell me."

"I dropped out of college and got married in September. He's a wonderful guy called Rick. Clean for two and a half years, the lead guitarist in the band. And I'm pregnant. I finally did it Martin! "

15

Summoned

Entrambi. It's the Italian word that means 'both' I quickly discovered. I'd always managed with *tutte due.*

I was in the wine bar at the end of the Via Nazionale in Cortona run by the wife of the former mayor. I was with Captain Cook who'd invited me for a sip. Captain Cook enjoyed a sip or six.

I said I'd join him but wouldn't sip, yet. As he sipped and I lipped, the lady from the *questura* came in. She's the most buxom wench in town with her jet black hair, ruby stuck lips and hourglass figure all perfectly balanced on high heels as she sways down the stone paved street. She's out of place in the law courts. She's a stray from an Irish pub in Benidorm or a professional tankard carrier at the Oktoberfest.

"He doesn't drink because he's sensible" she said to the Captain and asked me to follow her to the offices of the courtroom. Back down the street we go, the pair of us as I try to keep my eyes at eye level. Into the old *palazzo*, up the dark staircase and into her vast office. A large envelope sat on her desk. She got me to sign for it and asked me if Peter Ramsbottom could sign for his, and I told her Peter Ramsbottom no longer lived in Italy. I thanked her and returned to the *enoteca* and Captain Cook. Amongst the wine bottles, hams, cheeses, pastas, truffles and oils, I opened the large thick envelope and pulled out the enclosed papers. The first one I opened was heavily officially stamped and initialled.

Entrambi are accused of kidnapping the aforementioned girl from the above mentioned plaintiff's residence.

It's a good thing Big Pete isn't in Italy. He's accused of physically assaulting the plaintiff and causing serious and permanent injuries. I'm merely a co-kidnapper.

I say to the Captain that I think I'll have that glass of wine now and he gives me one of his broad smiles and passes me a full glass Vino Nobile di Montepulciano.

"So who's this Peter Ramsbottom?" enquires the Captain lighting a cigarette.

"He's a Brit who helped me out of trouble and back in again. This was a year ago. We'd got this Californian kid out of Italy and along the way, her Turkish boyfriend got a haircut. A very close shave as well. Pete was the barber. I was the driver, the getaway driver."

"Well where's this guy now?" Captain Cook is persistent.

"He went back to Blighty last winter. He drove back and crashed his car in the fog in Belgium, got a train back to London and a bus to Harrogate in Yorkshire where his girlfriend lives. She'd helped us in the coiffeur action. He rifled their joint bank account and ran off with her best friend. Nothing's been heard of him since."

"Nice guy to have as a friend." said the Captain.

Captain Cook is a sailor without a ship. He's a washed up galley chef, a reluctant landlubber who was blown off course, marooned ashore in this part of Italy just about as far away from the ocean as you can get. Captain Cook was a ship's cook and a Captain and he never lets you forget either. He's served on prawn fishing boats, cruise and cargo ships and even cooked in Alice's Restuarant.

Captain Cook is a cocktail of dollops of vintage Lee Van Cliff, splashes of ripe Wagner and a dash of some celebrity chef whose name slips me for the moment. On a good night after a few drinks, he actually reminds me of Burt Lancaster in a late career movie. You have to keep the lights low, though.

Captain Cook is German and hopefully still is. His grandfather (or was it his great grandfather?) was responsible for the First World War. The start of that conflict is always put down to a little bit of bother in the Balkans; that was just the detonator. Captain Cook's ancestor built the bomb. He was an engineer and he built the Kiel Canal which cut through southern Jutland separating Denmark from the new Germany, allowing German Dreadnaught class battleships to move from their bases in the Baltic into the North Sea unspied upon by the Danes (who hated the Prussians and immediately reported their naval manoeuvres back to Britain.) This gave the German navy a cutting edge over the British Fleet and, turbocharging the arms race, the alliances and counter alliances that would suck Europe and eventually most of the world into the war to end all wars. In a museum in Vienna, you can see the bloodstained uniform of the Arch Duke Franz Ferdinand, heir to the Austro Hungarian throne draped across the seat of the motor car in which he was assassinated. All that's missing is a photograph of Captain Cook's grandfather or was it his great grandfather?

Captain Cook bore that responsibility lightly. He was even, not so secretly, proud of it.

Eating dinner together one night in a little piazzetta outside a trattoria in Cortona, a jet fighter flew over in the night sky.

"There'll be another one in fourteen minutes." he said confidently. "The mayor's been onto them to stop this overhead flying."

Exactly one minute before a quarter of an hour was up, the night sky was ripped apart by another jet fighter. Captain Cook dissolved into one of his long, drawn out chortles with not even an "I told you so."

You learnt never to argue with Captain Cook. If the Captain's wrong he goes down with the ship. The Cook is always right.

As a boy he'd been a chorister. Hans Richter was his choir master and for him, J. S. Bach invented stereophony, placing half the choir in the north transept of the cathedral and the other half in the south.

When I first knew the Captain he was tall, dark and handsome with thick wavy hair, a moustache and an array of white even teeth which he shamelessly showed off when he laughed which he did often. Somewhere along the line of his chequered career he'd been a top executive for the German electrical multinational Braun, and had designed one of their more successful portable radios of which he still kept the prototype, but that was way back. When I last saw him he was in his sixties, gained a beer belly, gone grey and lost a couple of teeth, though he was still an imposing figure.

He drifted into town some twenty three years ago and started to get a reputation as a.) a volatile builder; he invariably fell out with his clients as they didn't want him to do things the way he said they should have been done so he usually stormed off the site losing client after client, and b.) a womaniser. He was handsome and single and there were available women. He vividly described, once, making love with a German lady in Umbria and she started to shake. Then the bed began to shake and the bedroom. The whole house was trembling! Just as he was mentally congratulating himself on his prowess, he realised that there was an earthquake. c.) A drinker: "Mornin Moi'n! How 'boud a sip?"

But he told good stories if you had the patience to listen to his lengthy, sermon-like deliveries.

W. C. Fields took a flask of liquor everywhere he went. He called it his pineapple juice. One day, someone stole it from him, quickly emptied it out and re-filled it with pineapple juice and put it back where W.C. could find it easily. When the actor next took a swig he yelled out "Who filled my pineapple juice with pineapple juice?"

When he was much younger, Captain Cook worked for an old boat builder in Provincetown, Massachusetts; a master craftsman, known locally as Flyer. Flyer had two sons, both left-handed Vietnam War vets who couldn't draw a crooked line between them, so Captain Cook was taken on to help complete the large scale model of the nineteenth century four masted sailing ship the 'Dorothea'.

Flyer was quite clear from the start: "No Micky Mouse jobs."

The Captain spent months painstakingly building the model while Flyer busied himself building boats.

Flyer wouldn't miss a thing. He'd come down from his high office where he was building a miniature rowing boat for his unborn grandson and check out the boat yard. "Did you clean that brush?" he'd shout to a painting apprentice.

One day, as Flyer was completing his grandson's boat, he bent a plank to a steep curve and was fixing it in place when Captain Cook said the stress of the curve would snap it. Flyer hit the fan and told the Captain to get on with his own work. It was just before the weekend when Flyer was going to New York for a master boatbuilders' reunion leaving Captain Cook to work through the holiday. Mid Sunday morning as the Captain was busy on the 'Dorothea', there was an almighty CRACK! and Flyer's plank snapped under the strain. Captain Cook spent the rest of the day repairing the piece, nursing it back into place and fastening it, then got on with his model. Flyer walked in on the Monday and carried on working as if nothing was amiss, but a couple of days later he said to the Captain "That was no Micky Mouse job you did there."

When the 'Dorothea' was complete, a model some ten metres long, fully rigged in all its detail, the town made a brass plaque to go alongside it bearing the maker's name, Captain Cook.

One New Year's eve when he was about twenty five, over thirty years ago, he sat in a chair in the living room of their house in Germany with his mother reclining on a sofa. He was her favourite son and, to his fury, she would call him Bearkin. That evening she did it on a full moon when he tended to run amok anyway.

On the wall behind the sofa hung a large painting of a Siberian snowscape into which you could have driven a sledge pulled by a full team of huskies and gone gliding off into the white infinity. The frame was ornate and richly gilded and the Captain always said it would fall off the wall as it was too heavy to be held on its three feeble hooks.

That evening she called him Bearkin once too often and he picked up the nearest object that happened to be an alarm clock and hurled it at her. For a few seconds, cogs, springs and wheels rained down on his mother. She told him to keep calm so he got up and opened a window to get some fresh air and a howling gale blew into the room scattering snowflakes and slamming a door. His mother jumped up from the sofa and screamed, bits of clock falling to the floor: there was a bat in the room! It had flown in when Bearkin opened the window and got crushed in the frame of the slamming door. Captain Cook closed the window, opened the door and the squashed body of the bat fell to the floor. He picked it up, opened the window again and threw it out.

"I can't take any more of this." his mother said. "Let's go down for dinner."

As they sat downstairs eating there was an ear shattering crash and they rushed upstairs and found the snowscape had broken from its hooks and smashed to the floor behind the sofa.

Captain Cook was a drifter for the last twenty years before he left Italy. He would move into the empty house below Cortona belonging to a psychologist nicknamed Gypsy, work on it until the Gypsy turned up, pack his bag, move out and drive in his car which doubled as his toolbox, to another empty house and repeat the process, breaking the rhythm with the occasional holiday in Thailand, or building cupboards and a fitted kitchen for a friend in New York who wrote opera scores, hacked computers and designed the software to run the New York subway system.

He spent the last few months in Italy staying in my house which was a mistake. Apart from the excellent meals, few of the promised jobs materialised in a haze of red, mulled wine and dominoes.

We played Maltese Cross obsessively. He was skilful and lucky at the game and on the whole won more than he lost. Just occasionally he would hit a losing streak and it would end up inevitably with a **splamshgaroong**! and the dominoes would hurtle across the table at me followed by the contents of his wine glass and two or three murder threats not far behind.

But it was with the meals he shone. Questions like the holocaust were subtly avoided. He refitted the gas plant from the outside *bombole* to the cooker, efficiently, emphasizing safety.

He taught me the secret in the kitchen: the stock. Stocks should be made the evening before, the shit boiled out of them before leaving them standing overnight and the coagulated fat scraped off in the morning. Then they are ready. The real secret within the secret is to fry up the meat first with the knuckles until all is a deep brown, then pour cold water onto the meat, making it contract, sealing in the juices. The full pan is placed back on the stove, a whole, unpeeled onion (to add colour), celery, carrots and garlic, added, bringing it to the boil and simmering it for hours. The last thing the cook does before leaving is to turn off the gas. Preparing dish after dish, the stockpot is constantly dipped into, a little here, a bit more there.

Captain Cook had this thing about food. If there was anything left over of an evening he would say: "Leave it and I'll fry an egg on it and have it for breakfast tomorrow morning." but he never did.

"I can't help it." he said, "I was brought up in the war and food was scarce. Hunger was our first fear."

His father spent six years in a concentration camp because he opposed National Socialism and survived because as an architect, he designed other concentration camps for the Nazis.

Together with his mother, brothers and sisters he lived in the largest house in their village in Bavaria. During the last winter of the war, with snow all around the house, there wasn't even the potato peelings or the outside leaves of cabbages to throw to the wild deer. One night, a huge stag came and rubbed his nose against the kitchen window and his mother opened it. The stag, normally so timid and shy, stood there with his great antlers, steam pouring from his nostrils asking - where's my food? Captain Cook's mother had to close the window on him as even firewood was scarce and it was freezing. As the war was drawing to a close and the allies approached, she called all her children into the kitchen, lined them up and with her face pale, handed each child five dried peas. She told them to put them under their tongues and let them dissolve before chewing and swallowing them. Afterwards she said there was one sugar lump for each of them - for dessert.

The next day, the Americans arrived and their house was commandeered for use as the headquarters of the commanding colonel and they were given U.S. Army rations and ate like they hadn't eaten for years. That's why he was loath to throw away any left-over food. But he chucked out my Cheddar cheese just as it was just getting ripe.

"How much shit are you deep in?" asked the Captain, as if he was plumbing the depths from the deck of his shrimper as it rode over a reef oceanwards on a fast ebbing tide.

"Up to my eyeballs" I replied.

"Well, keep it that way. Just don't go any deeper."

Great help you are, I thought.

The Captain got a job down in southern Italy so packed a bag and left. You can't have a ship with two captains on board so when he next called up, I told him he'd have to find another place to live. He called me up some weeks later with some drunken threats saying he knew I had a lot of legal problems but I was going to have even more soon. Last I heard he'd moved back to Germany and got a job as a security guard.

One thing, though, once the Captain had moved out of whatever house he was staying in, he'd leave every working knife in the kitchen razor sharp.

I took my legal problem to the lawyer I'd called up that night in Perugia a year back. I had little faith in him but felt stuck with him and he clung onto the case like a limpet. The hearing was set for a Wednesday morning in April.

He drove me to Perugia, parked in an underground car park and we walked to the court house, a large medieval stone palace right across the street in the old town and opposite the Alibi Bar!

Inside the building, I mentally switched off and went onto autopilot activating all my defence mechanisms.

Holy Mother. Holy, Holy, Holy, Holiest Mother. Holy Mother of whatever, whoever, whenever, why and wherefore. Holy Mother help. Help me, please.

I'm not one who goes along with all the stories they made up about your son. Look at all the people who got more than their fingers burnt because they listened to different versions of what He was alleged to have gotten up to and said and so on. I don't go to the theatres where your image is displayed and worshipped either so you have every right to ignore my pleas. But I know you carry a lot of weight around here. People look up to you. They respect you Holy Mother. So please listen.

I'm a writer which isn't strictly true but I'm being honest with you. I write. Let's put it that way. I try and write the truth. So many writers make up their stories. I wish I could make up stories but I just don't have the imagination, or the courage come to that. It must be so much easier to write when you have such a variety of lies to choose from. With the truth you have no choice. I write when I really have to. I write in the same way that I swim. I don't swim unless I really have to. But in certain critical situations if I don't swim I'll drown. That's when I swim. I write in the same way. I write to save my life. To save myself from being taken away and locked up. I'll be locked up not far from where I am now, where I'm asking you to intervene and help me as I need all the help I can get. Otherwise they'll shut me away very close to where Francis was locked up and had his epiphany. Where he changed his mind eight hundred years ago. Nearby to where he was imprisoned after his capture during another of those wars between the two cities that still watch each other today from their hilltop fortresses on either side of the river Tiber after all those years.

Holy Mother, I'd ask Francis again but I've already asked him something really important, extra special once, and he came up trumps so I can't really ask him again. I feel I've exhausted my credit with him. So I'm turning to you Holy Mother as I sit in this vast stone building with its vaulted ceiling and traces of frescoes of long ago scenes that once looked down upon the so called governors of this town who were really local mafiosi - families who ran things the way they wanted to run things and paid the fat French popes in Provence enough money extorted from the locals in taxes, ransoms and bribes to keep their holinesses reasonably happy and persuaded them not to interfere. Now this is the hall of justice Holy Mother. Now I'm sitting in this hall of justice surrounded by people who are about to judge me Holy Mother. They're going to decide just what hand I had in giving the gentleman sitting opposite me the scar he proudly displays down his right cheek. Holy Mother there are a lot of people in this room and I'm feeling very alone and there's a large steel cage over to one side where they put people a lot more dangerous than me when they come face to face with the law of the land just like I'm coming face to face with the law of the land, but outside the cage. Holy Mother many of these people I'm surrounded by wear black cloaks. The two men on either side of me wear black cloaks over their day to day clothes. They're lawyers. The one on my right is short, dark and has a balding saggy head with jowls like a Basset hound but I don't trust him as I would trust a dog if I trusted dogs which I don't. He hasn't done his homework and has only just put away in his pocket the rule book he's been studying the last two hours which hardly exudes confidence. Besides I can't stand his high squeaky voice. It grates so much you can't hear what he's saying. He's an ugly slimy little man.

On my left sits the lawyer representing the plaintiff, the guy with the scar sitting across the room, the man who accuses someone I know of painting that rather permanent tattoo on his clock, someone who isn't around to take the rap. So I'm going to get the full force of it all and for having a hand in kidnapping his girlfriend. Yes, I'm accused of snatching his girlfriend away from him in his house.

His lawyer, I suddenly notice, is wearing underneath his black cloak, identical clothes to myself. Orange corduroy jacket and trousers, a brown leather waistcoat and a white shirt with a red tie. Snap! Hey Holy Mother, did you set that up? Are you listening? Am I tuning in to your wavelength?

Various other men are perched on high chairs. They're wearing black cloaks too and they're writing notes. Television screens slung high up on the stone columns show coverage of all angles of the proceedings. Two ladies sit at a table typing away on strange looking typewriters. Across on the far side of the vast high-ceilinged room, below large leaded glass windows on a raised dais behind a large wooden desk overlooking the assembled throng sit three men. They are the magistrates, the judges. None of that trial by jury in Italy.

They too are robed in black, only what distinguishes

them from the rest of the cloaked men is that they're wearing on their heads sort of squashed black berets with red pompoms on top. They peer down at the people gathered together to make sure that justice is seen to be done. I'm not sure but I think the middle of the three judges, the head judge if you like, has a daughter that my sister once gave English lessons to. Holy Mother did you set that up too? We need all the allies we can get as this hall is full of unfriendly people. I have a feeling Holy Mother, that most of the lynch mob standing behind the wooden railing over there are hoping for blood. They've come to see me burn. They want me hung, briefly so I'm still wide awake, then they want to see me let down and slit open from chest to pubic bone, my guts ripped out and thrown on the blazing brazier before I'm cut into sections. They want my head on a steak so they can parade it through the streets of this city of despair. This city of violence. This city of vice. But, Holy Mother, with you on my side, with a bit of help from the man in the middle up there behind the desk wearing that funny hat maybe the mob are going to have a harder job than they expect. Maybe this isn't going to be plain sailing for them after all.

But, Holy Mother, I have to admit, right from the start, that I am guilty of what they are going to try and prove I'm guilty of. I knew from the start that that swarthy, good looking man of about forty with his black pony-tail was going to get a haircut he'd remember for the rest of his life. And I did steal his girlfriend from under his nose. I did that for her own safety. She was in bed with him one month after having organised bringing the barber to him for his short back and sides and spray painting his kitchen and his face to boot. He wouldn't have let her get off with that scot-free. He's a Turk. You know how they treat women Holy Mother? Yes I'm sure you do. They throw stones at them until they don't get back on their feet any more or they stand on their throats until they're writhing and the brothers and uncles join in; they set them on fire on the slightest suspicion of their stepping out of line. If there's any shadow of doubt they'll lock them in a room with a knife, a can of cooking oil and a box of matches, leaving them to decide. That way the family honour is restored Holy Mother, just in case you might have missed something. And the police will turn a blind eye Holy Mother because they recognise real men when they see them and they understand what honour means. That night he was going to fuck her again before he got his revenge. She'd come back and laid her head onto the block and even reached behind her head and pulled up her long hair to expose her thin white neck. Yes. He was going to hump her once more before throwing her to the wolves. Before he restored his honour. Yes he was. So I had to get her out. Do you see Holy Mother?

You have to remember Holy Mother what he did to her. All that violence and cruelty. She had to have been deeply hurt to want to see him damaged like that. What he got he got because he was due to get it if you see what I mean. He had it coming Holy Mother. Natural justice. Even those guys who picked us up and took us in and asked us questions confirmed he had something bad coming to him, if not quite as bad as what he eventually got.

So here I am Holy Mother and the man in the middle of the hatted trio up there behind his desk has just asked a young man (who I've never set eyes on before) who has just sat down on a chair in the centre of the room, what he saw the night of the alleged kidnapping? The young man is saying that he was sitting in his car with his girlfriend in the parking lot just next to this house when someone landed on the roof of his car causing his girlfriend to shriek. The next moment that person who was wearing a long white gown jumped down onto the bonnet of the car and then onto the ground and ran off among the other parked cars and no, he didn't get a look at his face and he couldn't say if he was that man sitting opposite. The man with the scar on his cheek. But he doesn't say that.

Now another young man has taken his place and I have seen him before. I spent an hour talking to him in his office the second night after we were pulled in to be questioned. While my friend was in the next room recounting his version of events, I told this new witness about the girl's school and some of her classmates and what they got up to and other people got up to with them. He told me about the town and the crime and how bad things really are and he's a Neapolitan. He comes from where they virtually invented organised crime. But, listen to this Holy Mother, he's saying he doesn't really remember much of that evening as it was nearly a year and a half ago and so much happens in his busy working life on a day-to-day basis, it's difficult to remember the details. Holy Mother he's being vague! He's on my side too! Is that you again doing what you seem to be doing so well?

Now the man with the hat turns and speaks to the guy with the pony-tail and the scar. He asks him his name, his place and date of birth. He asks him how long he's been in Italy. Then he gets to the nitty gritty and asks him what happened on the night shortly before Christmas the year before last in his house when he was interrupted whilst he was screwing an American teenager who one month earlier had sprayed his face with black paint while her friend held him in a neck lock and ran a Stanley knife up and down his rib cage before cutting his cheek, though he puts it all slightly differently. The guy with the pony -tail and the scar on his right cheek says he was at home with his girlfriend in the bedroom upstairs when there was a crash from the floor below. He quickly put on his nightdress and went to the top of the stairs and looked down. He saw two men below one carrying a huge knife. The man with the black hat and the red pompom asks him if either of these men are in this room and he points to me Holy Mother, which is fair enough as I was there that night. He says that I said "Go on. Kill him now. Finish the job." That wasn't true Holy Mother, I swear. I was always quite clear that he wasn't to be killed. But he's saying that was what I said and he understands English and he tells the court in English the words I never said. The next thing he did (he goes on) was to run back into the bedroom and jump out of the window. Now that I can believe. And I believe him when he says he can't read, that he's illiterate, but even he can't believe himself when he says they drove off in a Volkswagen Golf which had Swiss registration plates. That's my getaway car Holy Mother that he's referring to. He says he read the CH (Cofederazion Helvetique) displayed on its backside. Hey, this guy just said he can't read! And there's no CH on the back of my car. It has Zurich number plates but no CH. I can prove it. My lawyer sits watching all this. He should be up challenging that CH illiteracy point. Scarface then tells the court his relationship with the girl lasted one year. That's a load of cock! She arrived in Italy the beginning of July. She met him in Perugia early August. She flew back from the States to be with him early September. She left him late November and I kidnapped her after she'd gone back to him in late December. He not only can't read but his math is seriously debilitated too. Why doesn't my lawyer wake up and do something? The Turk then comes under some serious crossfire from the judge and he gets all tangled up in whys, whens and whats and as he's being verbally broadsided by the father of one of my sister's pupils, someone in the audience shouts out that their pal couldn't do anything at that point as he had to get himself to hospital. Whereupon the father of my sister's English patient throws the heckler out of the court; yeah! Listen to this Holy Mother: he's saying I wanted to marry her, a man nearly sixty marrying a teenager. Well hold on mate, I'm not even fifty three yet and she asked me to marry her not the other way round. My idiot lawyer is looking at me shocked, like my relationship with the teenager was anything more than a teacher- pupil thing never crossed his mind. He's so out of it. Style-less. The lawyers get to question the plaintiff. His lawyer doesn't have a question to ask but I think that's more to do with the fact that he's worried his client might dig an even deeper hole than he's already dug, rather than that we're dressed almost identically except for the black cloak. All my lawyer can come up with is to ask the guy what he does for a living and gets the reply that he sells chestnuts. My lawyer doesn't even have the sense to ask if he sells chestnuts all the year round. It's pathetic Holy Mother. I'm glad you're here looking over my shoulder if you're really here. The man with the funny black hat then says the court will adjourn, and consideration will be given to the written evidence it has in its possession after it has been translated. The court will reconvene in June. Holy crap! Those are the documents I handed over to the flying squad hoping to prove what a bastard he'd had been to her. They're going to be used as evidence against me. All today's little victories aren't going to be worth a flea's fart in a fridge if they contain what I think they contain. Well there's fuck all I can do about it. Just get on with what time I have left. The courtroom empties. It's lunch time. Kazim is greeted by his pals as they light up cigarettes outside on the street. Thanks Holy Mother for your help if it was you doing your best. I appreciate it, I really do. But I think I've done something that even you can't do anything about. Back then, after I got the girl onto to a plane and out of Italy, drove home from Milan and the cops arrived and asked all those questions, I handed over printouts of what I'd written, co-operating I 'd hoped. I now think I handed them an admission of guilt. I'll go home and check but I'm pretty sure of what I wrote. Holy Mother, I think I shot myself in the foot.

At home I checked what I thought I gave the plain-clothed policemen that winter's night over a year ago. The heading was "Penny Whistles" and on the second page I read "Tomorrow we're going to give that guy a haircut that he'll remember for the rest of his life."

Yes, we planned to cut off his pony-tail, his pride and joy, the symbol of his manhood. But Astrid wanted more. She wanted him to remember her for the rest of his life whenever he looked into a mirror.

I could have stopped it. I could have said just the pony-tail. Maybe a black eye or two but no more. But I didn't. I didn't because I believed he deserved worse. He abused her with an arrogance believing he was untouchable. There was no sexual jealousy on my part. Of that I was certain. When she started to get involved with him that summer it was a kind of relief as I'd agreed to marry her when she asked if I could help her stay in Italy, and that would only have led to tears which is where it's heading anyway.

I had to get the Penny Whistles files translated into Italian and give my retarded lawyer a copy though what he would make of it is probably not worth even thinking about. An Italian friend who had good English and who worked in the local courtroom from where I'd received the original indictment said he would translate it and when it was done I paid him with a crate of a good red wine.

I took a copy to the jowly creep in his tatty office above the bank. He read it through like he was reading an engrossing book. When he was done he looked up at me and squealed

"Perche?" Why did you give them this? *"Perche? Perche?"*

"Look, I gave it to them and they have it. *Capito*? It's no good asking why the stable door was left open. That's not going to make the fact that they've got it go away. We have to deal with it. *Capito?*"

I could see I was up shit creek and the pilot was totally out of his depth so I left him with his copy of Penny Whistles and went home and got drunk.

A week or so later I was walking down the Via Nazionale, the one horizontal road in town, where the locals do their *passagiata*, on my way to the bank when I saw the jowly Basset-hound's secretary approaching. She stopped in front of me, looked behind her briefly then said quietly and clearly:

"Get yourself a new lawyer. Your case is very delicate and my boss just isn't up to it. Understand? And you never heard me say this."

Then, with a faint whiff of Chanel number something-or-other and Marlborough Lights, like a shot off a shovel, she vanished.

Phut!

Just like that.

16

Michelangela

I went to my friend who'd translated the incriminating Penny Whistles and explained that my lawyer's very own secretary had advised me to find a decent criminal lawyer and he said he would ask his legal friends. A few days later he gave me the name and phone number of a certain *avvocato* in Perugia. I called his number and spoke to a secretary and made an appointment.

The address was familiar. The instructions to get to it were even more, though, I couldn't quite put a finger on it. I took a train to Perugia. Outside Perugia station at the bus ticket office the lady told me which bus to get and where to get off. It was early afternoon so the bus wasn't too crowded. It climbed the hill heading for the old town centre then swerved off to the right and went through an area I was totally unfamiliar with. Suddenly it came to a junction and took a right. I knew where we were. Just at the exit of the tunnel where Big Pete thought it had stopped raining. As I got my bearings I realised I'd passed my stop so rang the bell and the bus pulled in at the next request stop right outside the little red house! The very same space I'd parked in waiting for them to get the hairdressing business over and done with twenty one months ago.

I got off the bus warily, as I felt I was unwittingly returning to the scene of the crimes. I walked back up the street named after some date when Italy actually won a battle a hundred years ago more or less. Poor Italy. It didn't do very well in the twentieth century if you don't count soccer, the odd film, Piano, Dario and Lucciano. When you think back at how it was less than two thousand years ago. At the time of the Spanish emperors Trajan and Hadrian, the Roman empire stretched from just north of Carlisle to way further south of Cairo, from Moldavia to Morocco, from beyond Bilbao to behind Baghdad, but by the time of the battles of the belligerent Byzantine Belisarius, the blinking Romans blew away bit by bit the best blooming parts of it all to the bloody barbarians.

I found the building I needed on the corner just across the street from the tunnel. To the right of the large wooden door was a host of brass labels with lawyers' names on almost all of them. I found the door buzzer with the name of the one who I'd been told was a serious criminal lawyer and with whom I had an appointment and I pressed it. I was bang on time.

Going into lawyers' offices was a relatively new

experience so I hadn't built up the sorts of phobias one can accumulate, say when going to the dentist.

My lawyer's office in Cortona was just depressing. It's in a fine renaissance palace halfway down the main street and on the ground floor is the bank I use, the oldest bank in the world. Just down the high corridor is the tourist information centre so there are other reasons for visiting the building. On the *piano nobile* (the main floor) however it gets gloomy. The door to my lawyer's office is cheap and tacky. Inside is an apology for a waiting room: three chairs and a magazine rack containing a few tattered copies of way out-of-date faded and wrinkled coloured weeklies. The ceiling was interesting. The whole floor had been the main reception rooms of a once grand family. The ceiling was frescoed in a mid nineteenth century style with romantic landscapes and grotesque decorations. When the palazzo was divided up and sold off, hastily built walls were built chopping up the frescoes randomly. There were no pictures on the walls apart some framed certificates. The lawyer's private office had one wall lined with books. His secretary's room was as bleak, brightened up only by his secretary, a chirpy anglophile in her mid-thirties.

Now, I waited outside another lawyer's premises, just up the road from where I was accused of having committed a crime or two.

A voice crackled from the grille below the brass plaques and I gave my name. A clunk later and I was in a dark hall with several doors facing me and a stairwell. I pressed another buzzer on the door with the name of the legal offices where I had an appointment, and entered a bright room with smart smiling ladies behind a reception desk. Colourful prints hung on the walls. One lady took down my details, made a short phone call then led me along a corridor to a waiting area where she showed me to a chair and said I would be called up shortly. The magazines were relatively recent but I didn't have long to browse as a young man called my name and led me to a door at the far end of the corridor and I was shown into the new lawyer's office.

He stood up from behind his desk, not a tall man, about fifty with a hair so black that I would have sworn it was dyed. He had a friendly face and greeted me with a deep voice.

"Avvocado Macho. Signor Hutvood?"

Italians can't resist hadding an 'h' when there hisn't one and taking one away when there His. They don't even try doubleyous.

He bade me sit in one of two chairs in front of his desk. He made a quick phone call and asked me to wait a moment. I looked around the office. There was the obligatory wall of legal volumes but there were original paintings of landscapes, leather upholstered arm chairs and the smell of tobacco smoke.

The office door opened behind me and footsteps crossed the floor and a lady sat down in the chair beside me.

"Hi. I'm Michelangela. I'm a law student and I'm doing my internship with this practice. I speak English so I'm here to interpret for you. I'm told you speak good Italian but legal stuff is complex so I'm here to help."

She was a petite blonde and had a beaming smile. Smartly dressed and made up. She couldn't have been more than her mid twenties. Suddenly the whole sordid and depressing business of this court case brightened up. A lawyer with a deep voice and an interpreter who was bright and attractive. I felt a whole lot better and more confident about it all.

I told my story in Italian occasionally reverting to English when I hit a tricky patch and Michelangela would explain to the gentleman behind the desk. I handed over the Italian translation of Penny Whistles and we sat silently for several minutes while he took a cigarette from a packet, broke off a couple of centimetres, lit the rest, sat back and read the pages intently. When he'd finished he put them on his desk, looked at me and said

"You hit yourself in the foot didn't you."

"In English we say shot yourself in the foot. Yes."

"If you drive someone else to the bank and they rob it and you drive them away from the scene of the crime then you are also guilty of that crime." He looked at me seriously.

"I imagine it's just the same in British law. But do you think that can be proved from that text?" I asked.

"If his lawyer is bright he'll pick that up immediately. Who is his lawyer Michelangela? You've done some preparation on this case."

"Avvocato Monteverdi" she replied. "He's pretty smart."

"But the plaintiff contradicted himself several times in court, and lied too. He said he was illiterate then later that he read CH on the back of my car and there's not even CH on it. He said he'd known the girl for a year when I can prove that it was five months from when they met until when she left for the States the second time."

"Yes" he replied. "And he said he sold chestnuts for a living when everyone knows that's a very seasonal occupation."

"In the next hearing, can't you cross examine him and show him up to be a liar?" I asked.

"His lawyer, if he's as smart as we think, won't let him back in the court room. I don't want you there either. Once they've read this, they're going to cross examine you too and ask you details about the knife and the haircut."

I was partly relieved that I wouldn't have to sit through that ordeal again but angry with the other lawyer for having missed all those chances.

I said I would call them after the next hearing and we'd meet up again. Seeing Michelangela would make the experience far more pleasant.

That September I decided to leave my old farmhouse. It felt isolated and unsafe and I missed urban life. At first I thought of Siena but communications were poor by road and rail and it was a university city. Add that to tourism and you had one expensive place.

My lecturing job was a welcome relief from legal worries. For two hours four times a week I could totally concentrate on my audiences of mainly American adults and edutain them with

Italian art and history. As soon as I finished though,

the possibility of going to an Italian jail clanged down on my conscience like a falling portcullis.

I wanted to live in a town. Not Cortona. It was too small, too familiar. Somewhere new. Siena was pulling me but to drive to work along that road that could never decide whether it was a dual-carriageway or not was out. Rail connections too were pathetic. I believe the Sienese like it that way.

Walking round Orvieto with a small group of American tourists it suddenly occurred to me that this was the town I should move to. It had excellent rail connections, an hour by train to just below Cortona, an hour south to Rome and, most importantly, it was a natural fortress protected by high vertical tufa cliffs. It was a warm city and had a nice safe feeling. The people there were friendly and hospitable and there was that magnificent cathedral.

The Sunday after the penny dropped, I took the train to Orvieto, the funicular cable car from the rail station up to the old city and explored. Walking up the Corso Cavour, the street that runs from the funicular station to the town centre, lined with houses and shops built out of the honey-coloured volcanic tufa rock giving a golden glow to the place, I saw a notice *Casa in Affito,* house to rent and a phone number. I called but there was no reply.

I didn't find anything that day but returned the next Sunday and called the number again. A lady answered. I asked about the house and she gave me the address and said I should go and look at it from the outside and if it looked promising, to call her back.

I asked directions and walked back down the Corso,

went through an arched tunnel and into a small piazza with two and three storied houses all around, with well kept terraces and loggias of cascading flowers. A white Persian cat sat licking itself in the sunshine. The address she gave me was up a short flight of steps which I climbed to a heavy wooden door. I couldn't see much through the window next to it so went back down to where the cat was sitting and looked up at the house. There was one more floor above the entrance and a French window led out from it onto a small empty terrace. I called the lady back and said I'd be interested in seeing inside. She said she'd be about fifteen minutes so I waited in the piazza in the sun petting the white cat. A lady came round the corner and I thought that couldn't be the lady I'd phoned so recently. She smiled and pointing to the cat said she was called Penelope. The lady lived in the house at the top of the piazza. I told her I was looking at the house for let and she said if I needed anything they were there.

Some minutes later a very different lady walked into the piazza from the Corso. She was about my age, short, heavily made up with a flashy coat, and her hair mounded up like a beehive. She blinged with jewellery.

She introduced herself and we shook hands. She unlocked a steel mesh door at the foot of the outside staircase. I'd not noticed it thinking it wasn't part of the property. I followed her into a low cool dark ground floor room lit by a small window and the light from the door. The walls were bare tufo stone. She clipped across the cream floor tiles to the far corner and climbed a spiral staircase. It was getting better by the minute. We emerged into a small kitchen having an opening into a small dining/living space with the door leading out to the steps and a large window next to it. She opened a door to a small bathroom then led me up a terracotta staircase into the darker back bedroom. The walls were painted sky blue with white clouds. Liveable with I thought. The second bedroom was considerably lighter with a floor to ceiling window leading out onto the terrace with ornate cast iron railings. A tiny washroom and toilet completed the layout. Perfect I thought. I asked her how much was the rent? 680,000 Lire a month she said. 800,00 was my limit so I was well inside it. I said I'd take it and would pay a deposit immediately. By the time we'd got to the bottom of the stairs she was saying 700,000 thinking I was a rich foreigner. I said she'd said 680 so we settled on 690,000.

The next weekend I drove down to Orvieto with a few basic things, and the landlady, Signora Micci and I signed a rental contract at a local notary's office.

Over the next few weeks I transferred furniture, kitchen stuff, books and pictures and settled into my new home. I discovered that Orvieto had the bar reputed to be the second best in Italy and two local cinemas, one with small divans in the auditorium.

By the time I was feeling at home, another court hearing passed. I drove to Perugia this time and squeezed my Renault into a back street park space and walked to the lawyer's office building.

Avvocato Macho and Michelangela told me about the hearing. My text Penny Whistles had been read in court and proved to be pretty damning but that would, in the end, depend on the magistrates. The final hearing was set for mid December. Michelangela spelt it out clearly: damage limitation was the best we could go for. I tried to explain that we wanted to give the guy the memorable haircut as his pony-tail was his pride and joy. With it, Astrid told me, he said he could have any woman in Perugia. We wanted to metaphorically castrate him. They didn't even bite let alone swallow that line. It was then that I realised I was totally at the mercy of their idea of what they thought they could get me off, and what they thought they couldn't. Deep down, though, I knew they were right.

The final hearing was in mid December. Macho gave a deep voiced delivery and ended with "There can be various interpretations of 'I love you'" and I wondered what the hell he was on about. I'd kept old squeaky jowly on my legal team and when he got up and squeaked away I didn't even bother listening to the content of his summing up. The magistrates withdrew for about forty minutes. Macho smoked a cigarette in court which I thought was cheeky. Michelangela and I smoked outside.

The magistrates re-emerged from their deliberation and the courtroom hushed. Big Pete got one year and one week suspended.

I got one year suspended. I guess we'd got off lightly sentence-wise. I was condemned to pay old lover boy 15 million lire in damages and his legal costs. Big Pete got the same, but of course, wasn't around to take that rap. It could have been a lot worse and it could have been a lot better for me, however Big Pete had it coming but was far enough away not to be bothered.

Michelangela gave me a smile and a shrug and one raised eyebrow, whatever that meant. I took her and Macho out for lunch. Macho then, only then, asked me the question:

"*Allora professore,* tell me, why did you hand over that Penny Whistles document to the flying squad?"

"I was trying to help the cops and I was tired. I hadn't slept for two nights. A few glasses of wine probably didn't help." I said looking out through the restaurant window across the Tiber valley to recently-earthquaked Assisi. I'd seen that video footage of the vault crashing down on the group of people killing four, and the dust tsunamiing up the nave of the upper basilica of San Francesco, a haunting trailer of things to come.

Macho said we could appeal and Michelangela said that could take four years to go through the system. I said I was all for burying my head in the rubble. I paid the bill like I was William Gatespeare on a rare night out painting la ville rouge.

"There's something I want to know too *avvocado.*" I said to Macho."How come a known drug addict, a petty criminal with no documents can be *intoccabile,* untouchable?"

Michelangela cut in. "He got all his documents by prosecuting you, by the court case."

"Good. I'm glad he got something out of it." I said, wondering where the money to fix his face was going to come from.

"To answer your question, *simplice,*" said the

lawyer, wiping the last of the *spaghetti con vongole* from his moustache. "He's a police informer."

17

Civil suit

I know where I went wrong. I know what I should have done long after I didn't do it. Hindsight has such a sick way of reminding you of your bad decisions. But, as Groucho Marx said, it ain't worth a dime.

I know exactly when I should have gotten out, when I should have done a runner. I'd just sold my farm, paid my ex-wife to her satisfaction, banked enough to more than cover my overdraft and at dinner with the estate agent, her companion, the purchaser, her husband and my ex-wife, I was handed a thick envelope under the restaurant table. It was about ten centimetres thick, twenty five centimetres long and twelve centimetres wide. It contained pieces of paper coloured purple, yellow and green. That's when I should have finished the meal, put the envelope into my leather case, gone back to the hotel, slept with my hand clutching the envelope under my pillow, woken up, put the envelope into the leather case again, had breakfast, gone to the dealership in the valley and bought myself a brand new camper van with a discount for cash, driven up to the old farm, picked out the stuff I wanted to keep, made a pile of the rest, dowsed it in kerosene and lit it, driven down to Orvieto, parked my camper in the stadium car park, removed my leather case with its contents, locked the camper carefully, gone to my little house in its laid back little square, given Penelope a scratch behind her ears, climbed the steps, unlocked the door and let myself in, gone upstairs and stowed the leather case and contents in the secret cupboard in the little bathroom, gone down to the kitchen, poured myself a large glass of cold Orvieto Classico wine, put on Mozart's clarinet concerto and had a good laugh, a deep down belly laugh. The next day I should have packed up the camper, called the landlady to say I was leaving and the keys would be at the bar around the corner and driven north west out of Italy as fast as I could.

But I didn't.

I lived in the little house in Orvieto for six years. Astrid and I lost touch with each other soon after I moved in. I'd asked her to ask her wealthy grandmother to help with my forthcoming legal expenses. She told me she hadn't even told her grandmother anything about what had happened in Perugia as it would have given her a heart attack. We'd both gently hung up on each other.

The Italian legal system ground through its snail like creaking procedures. I was hoping it would last beyond the five years of the statute of limitations. As the years passed I was gradually getting used to the black cloud hovering above my life.

Six months short of the deadline the court of appeal rejected my case which was what Macho said was the probable decision after he'd squeezed every euro out of me that he could. I was warned that Kazim could go after me in the civil courts now, and that if I bought another house, I should put it in someone else's name.

I did find a little gem of a house just outside Bolsena next to the lake of the same name. It had everything on my mental list of my ideal house and something extra special, a wood fired pizza oven in the kitchen. As soon as I had that envelope safely back in fortress Orvieto, I drove down to the agents in Bolsena and we made a deal.

The complications over extra taxes and the fact that my daughter (in whose name I wanted to put it) lived in California, meant in the end, that the house had to be registered in my name.

One week before moving out of the little house in Orvieto, the phone rang.

"Martin? Hi this is Astrid."

"Hi Astrid. You caught me just as I was about to move house. Just in time. How are you?"

"I'm good. I remarried and have a small son. I'm a third year student studying micro-biology at college and loving it. What's with you?"

"Well, like I said, I'm just about to move to a house near a little town beside the largest volcanic lake in Europe. The case with Kazim is finally over. I got a one year suspended sentence and had to pay Kazim quite a lot of money and we know how he'll be spending that."

"Martin, I want to thank you again for what you did. You saved my life. When you've moved, e-mail me your new phone number and we'll keep in touch. Don't forget we're pals for life."

"I won't. Thanks for calling. That was good timing."

Astrid has a knack of bobbing back to the surface of my life again just when I least expect it.

With the help of friends I cleared out the old farmhouse in the hills behind Cortona. Sad to leave it but hopefully the new owners could throw a small fortune at it and get it into shape. I'd struggled but it was just too much. I cleared out the little house in Orvieto too. They say the three most traumatic events in life are a death in the family, divorce and moving house. Divorce for me was easy. All those thousands of people who go to Venice for their honeymoons or for a romantic break, or to patch up a leaky marriage, well I got divorced in Venice. Easy and cheap. Moving out of two houses into another one made up for it.

Astrid maintained contact. Her e-mails described a crumbling second marriage but an ever more successful academic career. She'd entered the PhD program at her university and was doing original and ground-breaking research. She adored being a 'mom' too. Somehow all that shit in Perugia and the aftermath seemed to have been worth it.

Eighteen months into my new life I got a rude awakening. Sitting in the local internet cafe one morning, a man walked in and asked for Martin Hutvood. The lady at the bar pointed to me and the gentleman walked over and handed me an envelope. I didn't have to sign for it or anything and he left.

Inside that brown envelope was a document saying that as I hadn't attended the opening hearings of the civil action being brought on me by a certain gentleman, the court was putting a fifty thousand euro injunction on my house.

Fuck. Kazim's back.

I called up Michelangela and we made an appointment.

I used to love Perugia. Not as much as Siena but up there with Arezzo. I don't much like the painter called Perugino. His women all have the same faces. In the National Gallery of Umbria there's a brilliant painting of ships by Fra Angelico and that mysterious Annunciation by Piero della Francesca with all those interpretations about virginity and hymens. The best thing is the fountain in the piazza outside. Father and son, Nicolo and Giovanni. Father came from the south, from the court of Federico II in Pulia where he'd been encouraged to look at pagan sculpture by that enlightened patron. This duo really were forerunners of the renaissance. Now they're restoring the fountain in Perugia and the odds are they're going to ruin it for keeps. Sad really. When the Italians get it right they really get it perfect. Trouble is when they don't they screw up big time.

Now Perugia is full of ghosts from those nights back in that winter nearly nine years ago. I didn't look at the art any more. I went in, did what I had to do then got the hell out. I dreaded bumping into Kazim. That smug look on his scarred face as he sauntered down the courtroom basking in his moment of glory. I bet he never had that scar removed. I reckon he uses that along with his pony-tail to pull birds. Sexy scarface. He's probably secretly proud of it and has a repertoire of stories about how he got it.

Michelangela's office was down a narrow street between the cathedral and the Etruscan gate. You couldn't get away from this history everywhere. She had graduated and now was a fully fledged lawyer. She shared the office with her sister and some other lawyers. The building was full of lawyers and knowing Perugia I knew they were kept busy.

I was shown in to a large room mostly filled with a wooden boardroom sized table and leather backed chairs. Two walls were completely covered with book shelves containing the usual anonymous volumes. One wall had framed posters of aerial photographs of Venice and Florence and the fourth wall's two windows looked out onto the shuttered dusty building opposite which was close enough to touch if you were bored enough to reach out.

Michelangela came in through a side door. She hadn't changed one bit but then why should she have? We both sat down and I handed her my latest Valentine's card and the injunction. She read them silently then left the room to make a phone call. She returned and said that the court had held the opening procedures when the lawyers present their clients. I hadn't been represented so they'd slapped an injunction on my house. I remembered an earlier registered letter I'd not reclaimed. My daughter was staying with me and we were travelling. Michelangela said she'd just called the court secretary and there was still time to get back on track but she was clear that the civil court wasn't going to overturn the penal court's decision. It was going to be damage limitation. We had to keep damages and costs as low as possible.

Over the following months we met regularly. I learnt about the legal extent of damages, physical and moral, on a scale from one to fifteen. Kazim was claiming maximum in both categories. Michelangela dug out original medical records when Kazim went to hospital bleeding from the face. She also got his methadone records which was something Macho and that basset hound of a lawyer in Cortona denied ever existed. We steadily built up a gloomier and blacker picture of what the whole thing was going to cost me. And that was before any legal fees.

My little house by the deepest, largest volcanic lake in Europe, with its pizza oven in the kitchen and its tiny terrace looking across an olive grove to the castle on the hill began to feel like a trap. I began to appreciate what people caught in negative equity felt, or worse, property ladder climbers who'd borrowed over their heads on the bottom rung, climbed a step or two only to have the ladder pulled out from under their upwardly mobile dreams. I couldn't sell the house with that judicial injunction so had to sit it out until the house was inevitably put up for a judicial auction like the properties and businesses I read about on the posters on the hoarding right outside my house along with the funeral notices and posters announcing the latest Russian circuses, local fish eating contests, which motorists stopped to read leaving their global warming, iceberg melting SUVs churning out diesel fumes in through my kitchen window. My dream house would be knocked down to a bidder or ring of bidders for enough to pay Kazim's legal damages, the legal and court's costs. This was called stripping, no, ripping the shirt off your back. It somehow took the edge off having a wood fired pizza oven in the kitchen of the little house beside the largest volcanic lake in Europe with a view from the terrace across an olive grove to a medieval castle on a hill.

Michelangela drew up a new strategy. We would apply for the injunction to be lifted. She would put the case as one of dishonesty on the part of the plaintiff, a registered drug addict, against honesty, a man with a track record of working with the local community educationally which had a positive trickle down effect on the local economy etc. etc.

She said she wanted me in court personally. We went to the hearing in the market place of the civil courts, the maelstrom of smart cocky lawyers on their cell phones and bursting briefcases briefing the hollow eyed desperate defendants or perplexed plaintiffs milling about above the main post office, a building not nearly as interesting as the penal court house just across the street and down the road from the Alibi bar.

There was a scrum in the office with lawyers crushed up against the desk of who I took to be the clerk. He was the judge I learnt when we sat in front of him and Michelangela put our case passionately, compared to the plaintiff's lawyer who was so satisfyingly feeble that we won the hearing! The plaintiff's lawyer stormed out.

Michelangela's a star. She's beautiful, laughs a lot, is extremely intelligent and wanted to get me off as lightly as possible. When we left the judge's office she collected her coat and I held it for her as she threaded in her arms. Her long fair hair was trapped inside her coat collar so with a sweep of my hand I swept it out and that was the extent of our physical intimacy apart from the formal peck cheek against cheek with which we greeted each other. She once had a Scottish boyfriend so could reel off "Thire's ah moose loose aboot the hoos."

The plaintiff's lawyer appealed the decision. Michelangela and I discussed strategy. She'd moved offices now and she and her sister shared a spacious corner room in a large building at the top of the September Street. I'd worked my way steadily up that street from Kazim's red little house to Macho's offices and hopefully finally to Michelangela's studio.

I told her I had a very special friend who was married to a man whose father was high up in the Italian judicial hierarchy. We went back a long way. I never asked her for any favours before. We were unconditional friends. But now, as Michelangela said, we needed to go into the court armed to the teeth.

Ellie is a true European. That's all you can say regarding her nationality. She comes from so many countries and cultures and speaks so many languages that I bet she has at least five passports. We'd met years ago when she was working tables at a *spaghetteria* opposite the trattoria where I often had lunch. I don't remember exactly how we met but when we did we got on like a flamethrower. Her eyes sparkled behind her spectacles and she had a contagious laugh. We really got to know each other well when she asked me to break her arm.

It was mid winter and she was out of a job, had just fallen in love with an Italian man and desperately wanted to stay in Italy. She had health insurance and she wanted the money so she asked me to break her arm. Actually she ordered me. She was house sitting for some Germans but couldn't afford heating oil or firewood and it was ffffreezing when I called by with my two hammers. She led me into the kitchen and sat herself down by the kitchen table, rolled up the sleeve of her left arm and laid it on the table like dinner. I'd brought a rubber headed tilers' hammer to protect her skin and a steel headed killer hammer for the hit. I put the head of the rubber hammer onto her forearm, took a deep breath then gave it a mighty whack with the killer. She winced, moved her fingers like they were stiff, shook her head and said it hadn't broken and I should have another crack at it but harder this time. The second hit severely shook the table. She looked at me, laughed and said that was it and told me to get the shit out of there.

I met up with her a few days later. Her arm was in a sling but there was no plaster-of-Paris. She shook her head and said it was only badly bruised but thanked me anyway. Shortly after she got offered a job, got together with her Italian man and eventually they got married and had a delightful multi-lingual family. So when you want to say good luck to someone, don't say break a leg as they say to actors before a show. Say break an arm. Or at least give it a try.

Ellie's house, by sheer coincidence, had been built years before by my brother. I went to see her and we had lunch and talked about her children, my daughter, work and the price of eggs. Then I asked her to speak to her husband's father about my case. Ellie had known Astrid and a broad outline of the events while Astrid was in and out of Perugia. Without hesitating Ellie agreed. She said that that guy in Perugia was evil and she had no qualms about it at all.

"Besides," she said, as she gave me one of her eye smiles through the lenses of her specs, "you've already paid far too much for what will almost certainly be the most expensive sex of your life. I don't want you to have to pay any more."

Ellie did talk to him and I'll never know what her father-in-law said or did, but the hearing over the plaintiff's lawyer's appeal against the lifting of the injunction on my house came up. I went with Michelangela back to the same old market building above the post office, across the road from the penal court and just down the road from what used to be the Alibi bar.

Ancient Romans, in their forums built huge long buildings with a main central space, columns and arches dividing it on either side from slightly smaller spaces with a row of windows high up to let in more light and semi-circular recesses at strategic points that housed statues of the latest imperial deities. Here they held their courts of law, their money changers' stalls, their stock markets and generally met to discuss the latest talk of the town. These basilicas as they were called became the architectural models for the later Christian churches as they were untainted by paganism. Well, the civil courthouse in Perugia resembled a Roman basilica, not architecturally but in noise, activity and general chaotic comings and goings.

When our turn came up Michelangela and I, along with the enemy's lawyer, the tall thin lady without a smile in the world, were ushered into a large room and we sat down at a table opposite two men and a woman. They looked like members of the parish council with no airs of judicial authority at all. They were dressed casually and one man lolled on his chair with his elbows on the table like he couldn't think of a more boring way to spend his precious time.

The thin lady began, and droned on monotonously. Then it was Michelangela's turn and she put on a class act. My mind switches off content in Italian courts of law I'd discovered, so I didn't understand a quarter of what she said but it was the way she said it. Madonna! She really ripped into old skinny flintstone sitting next to her for suggesting that I attended the hearings because I was unemployed so couldn't afford to pay the damages so my house would have to go to a judicial auction to retrieve damages and costs. I knew she said that because Michelangela'd briefed me before the hearing that that was part of what she was going to say, along with all the other things she said. When she stopped and we were dismissed by the three tennis umpires, the enemy's lawyer left the court like she knew she hadn't a hope in hell. I didn't even have to fall back on my secret weapon.

Ten days later Michelangela e-mailed me:

Just to tell you: Appeal won! Plaintiff's request rejected.

Speak to you soon. Michelangela.

My house was now free to be sold.

A few weeks after the hearing the agent selling my house rang the door bell and asked me to accompany her to her office. She sat me down and said the lady she'd shown the house to yesterday had made an offer. When I heard the amount which was not as much as I was asking but more than I paid for it, I said I needed a couple of days to think it over. She said take your time. I called Michelangela and asked if I could come and see her as I had some important news. We fixed to meet at five. I drove up the Tiber Valley to see her and by the time I got to the caravan dealership below Perugia, as I had an hour to spare before the appointment, I popped in.

That's when I discovered America.

18

Discovering America

I'd always loathed campers, or auto caravans, whatever you want to call them. They're slow, cumbersome and clog up traffic on winding narrow roads during the summer months.

Just like suburban householders, camper owners display all the trophies of their material success. Besides the vehicles themselves, the newest, state-of-the art body work is essential. What's carried on top is just as important for these one-up-man ships as it's visible for all to see: surf boards, preferably several of them in one or two stacks; complex radio and TV aerials and dishes to show you might be getting away from it yet you're still staying in touch.

What goes on the back is especially important. Anyone following a camper is going to have a considerable amount of time to examine and assess what's racked on the back. Mountain bikes, racing bikes, foldable mini-bikes, scooters, motorbikes, anything with two wheels gets to go on the back of the campers and invites speculation about the people inside; husband and wife, youngish, kids, elderly and retired? To be really king of the road you really need a brand new Mercedes powered Hymer camper towing a trailer carrying a smart car with a small yellow D on the registration plate.

The best camper combo I ever saw was an elderly Fiat ARCA towing a trailer carrying a1957 yellow Fiat 500, the classic *cinquecento*, behind it.

After over twenty years of living in a remote old stone farm house, as old as America (it had 1776 carved into the stone lintel over one window), up in the hills above one of the oldest towns in Europe, then being plagued by a religious sect of a neighbour (whom we eventually managed to help evict), I moved to a small town house in an equally ancient city but the house was rented and no way could I buy it. When I sold the farm I bought a little house down by Lake Bolsena. My immediate neighbour who owned the olive grove I looked out over from my tiny upstairs terrace and up to the medieval castle on the hill beyond, was an eighty something year old lady. She was as strong as an ox and watched every bit of agricultural activity on her extensive property. Three years after I moved there, she died and her nephew inherited the property. He had four dogs and they'd come and bark at me as I sat on the little terrace. Because of the nature of the layout of the land in relation to the house, one dog would climb onto the roof of my house and bark down at me!

The town, as towns will, had rats. Like the dog, rats found their way onto my roof and down onto the terrace. I disturbed a huge brown bugger hiding in the cool shade of my Lebanese succulent plant. The bathroom was immediately behind and slightly below the terrace and I kept a hosepipe attached to a fitting on the cold water pipe beneath the sink which ran out through the bathroom window to water my beloved wisteria, jasmine and other plants. One night, coming into the bathroom, I disturbed another giant brown rat scurrying up the hosepipe in a hurry to get out of the window.

In the square outside my house (square it wasn't - a wide open tarmac car park), there was a row of large garbage bins at the end of someone's garden. It was about one hundred metres from my house and many mornings as I walked to town carrying my plastic bag of garbage, I could throw it directly into the garbage truck as it emptied the bins. One day, workmen began clearing an area across the road on a small grassy park under some plane trees, closer to my house, where owners walked their shitty little dogs though signs said it was clearly forbidden. I asked the workmen what they were making? A new place to put the garbage bins I was told. Apparently the owner of the garden where they were had complained enough of the smell, the cats and - the rats. After a few days, work under the trees stopped. A week or two later an area of the road outside my house bordering the wall of the olive grove, where I used to park my car was fenced off with the red and white tape strung from iron poles. I was told that the lady living in the house next to where it was planned to move the garbage bins had complained. She lived in Rome and only came to her Bolsena house some weekends. So the municipal authorities decided they'd build a place across the road next to the house of the Englishman who wouldn't make a fuss.

It was time to move. But there was an injunction on my house. I was trapped with the garbage and the rats! With some fine legal rhetoric and some behind the scenes judicial muscle, the injunction was lifted and the house sold, just before construction work on the new garbage bin location begun.

Another of the special details of that precious little house was the flag flying on the mast on the tower of the medieval castle. I could lie in bed in the morning and see the flag and get a good idea what the weather was going to be like that day. Soon after I eventually left, the flag pole was replaced by a mobile phone tower.

Over the months before Michelangela and Ellie between them managed to clear the injunction on the house, I'd begun to have a change of heart about those campers. Slowly it dawned on me that the ability to up sticks and move somewhere else when a particular neighbour became a pain in the arse, or a plague of rats threatened, or just a mammoth bill for damages and legal fees was going to see my home put up for a judicial auction and I'd lose everything, had some distinct advantages.

Campers gradually became an option, a means of escaping rats and garbage of all shapes and sizes. I began to spend serious time looking at what was on offer at local dealerships. I couldn't ever afford a new one. I wasn't even sure if I'd ever be able to afford a used one but I wanted to be prepared. I checked websites. If I found myself stuck behind a camper crawling up the hill of hairpin bends between Orvieto and Bolsena, I'd be in no hurry to overtake. It was a chance to make mental notes about sizes, extras, speeds and other little details I'd never considered before. Over the year or so from when I swung from being an anti-camper maniac to a pro-camper fanatic, I'd built a clear mental picture of what I wanted and how much it was going to cost.

Joshua Slocum was an old Canadian sea dog. He'd retired to the United States after a long and colourful career at sea when sailing ships we're still abundant and hadn't been replaced by steam ships. In the 1890's, he came across a derelict shrimper lying on the mudflats at Fairhaven, Massachusetts, on the north east coast of the United States. He saw in this boat the perfect lines that years of looking had trained him to recognise. He purchased the wreck, rebuilt her plank by plank, kept her name Spray and sailed her single-handed round the world. He was the first person to do that and wrote a classic travel book about it. In 1909 on one of his later voyages he sailed off and never returned. What happen to Joshua Slocum and the Spray has remained to this day a mysterious topic of maritime speculation.

The mental list of requirements for my ideal camper evolved slowly and eventually boiled down to four essential points:

1. Price ceiling 15,000 euros.

2. Sleeping space with windows above driving cab.
3. Largest possible bathroom.
4. Neutral upholstery and interior design.

I could have added low mileage, character, ample storage space, and so on, but those four points were my basic criteria.

Location was important. On the internet I'd found what appeared to be a perfect camper in Genova. What if it wasn't quite so perfect by the time I'd made the journey up half of Italy to check it out? Ownership was important too. One owner would be perfect. Two maximum. Some campers were used as brothels and were parked in lay-bys alongside busy roads like the N448 between Orvieto and Todi. They were the workplaces of the Italian prostitutes who'd mostly past their sell-by dates. The campers were the only advantage they had over the younger, sleeker Nigerians, Romanians or Estonians who worked directly off the road with their backs to the river Tiber valley and hilltop towns with vineyards and cypress trees as a backdrop to their slavery. I didn't want to buy a mobile whorehouse.

When the house agent told me of the offer on my house it was around midday. I called Michelangela and we made an appointment to meet in her office at four. It took just over an hour to drive to Perugia. By the time I'd got to within sight of the towers of that city up on the hill, it wasn't even three. With more than an hour to spare, I decided to call in at the camper dealership I'd visited a few times on some of my previous trips to Perugia. I pulled off the SS 3 and over onto a minor road that ran back to where the rows of brand new campers were parked that you could see from the main road.

Immediately as I walked through the gate, in front were two lines of parked used campers. One of the salesmen greeted me and showed me the first camper in one row. It didn't fit any of my four requirements.

But the second one did. Right from the moment I saw it, this one had something special about it. The salesman showed me in. The interior had a warm, golden, light wood finish to the cupboards and shelves. The floor had a surface of fake terracotta tiles and the upholstery of the bench seats was a neutral, tan corduroy. There was a double sleeping space over the driver's cab with a small side window and a rare large window facing forwards. One side of the rear interior had bunk beds and the other side an ample sized bathroom compared to some of the cubby holes I'd seen. In the centre was a table, two bench seats by a long panoramic window and on the other side the kitchen area. The salesman thumped the ceiling to emphasise how solidly it was built. I checked the kilometres: 96,000. How many owners? One. What year was it matriculated? 1988.

How much was it?

15,000 euros.

Joshua Slocum had found his Spray.

Only this time the Spray hopefully wouldn't need to be completely rebuilt. It would keep its original name too. On the outside, about half way up the rear of the bodywork on either side, in an unidentifiable typeface was stencilled boldly in large black letters 'AMERICA New Deal.'

I spoke to the owner of the dealership and he accepted a small deposit on America to hold the sale for one week. It was December so campers weren't exactly selling like hot cakes and flying out the gate. I drove on to Perugia and Michelangela's office.

I told her of the offer on the house and the camper and that I could now start a countdown to leaving Italy.

She'd never actually condoned that I was planning to do a runner, but she never advised me against it either. I got clear implicit signals, though, that no one was going to come after me if I did.

I was planning to go to Spain.

There weren't many choices open. Britain was out. Climate and expense. Greece I'd known a bit but there was nothing there to draw me other than ancient ruins and I'd seen more than enough of those in Italy. France was a possibility but Spain had been flashing on my radar for some years. The language wasn't too different from Italian in which I was fairly fluent. Friends said it was cheap. There was a sizeable British community along the southern coasts and, of course, there was the sun. In Spain they ate tapas; lots of small, savoury samples and I was tired of the big helpings of pasta. I took the pasta/tapas anagram as a positive sign. Plus I knew friends of friends in Murcia and a cousin's daughter had married a Spaniard and they lived in northern Spain. Besides I knew a bit about the Spanish Armada, more about Diego Velàzquez and I had an earbug of that hit by the Tomato Chicks.

I asked Michelangela to begin to draw up my bill for her work. I'd avoided paying Kazim's lawyers. The daily compound interest on his bill by the time I'd discovered America would have paid off most of the national debt of Chad. I half paid the jowly old fart I'd taken on at the beginning, asked for a receipt of payments to date, then stopped further payments. I considered he'd already been grossly overpaid for his incompetence. Registered letters spluttered for a few weeks, which I ignored. Then he gave up. I'd paid Macho every penny he'd asked for, five payments in all, and I'd only had a receipt for the first. I used this fact not to pay the civil lawyer Macho'd assigned me who'd just got in the way trying to earn his fees during the sale of the farmhouse.

Michelangela had done three times as much research in the case than all the others put together. She'd traced the hospital records of when Kazim was first admitted that night yonks ago. She'd taken down a detailed report from the doctor on duty that night. She'd found Kazim's methadone records too, something Macho and old floppy jowls denied existed because they never took the trouble to go find out. She'd taken independent legal medical advice as to the extent of the physical and psychological damages the plaintiff was claiming and assessed them in the light of legal precedents.

But, most of all, during all our court hearings, she'd fought for me like a tigress. Michelangela was going to get every euro she asked for.

All that remained was to complete the sale of the house.

The agents set it up perfectly. They'd liaised with Michelangela and had done their homework with their own lawyer. They prepared all the papers meticulously so the purchaser knew exactly where she stood legally. We did the preliminary contract and the purchaser paid the deposit which was a conclusive commitment on her part. If she withdrew from the sale she would lose her deposit. If I pulled out I would have to return her deposit doubled! It was now a question of when the final payment would come through. The end of February was the deadline.

The director of the camper dealership near Perugia said he couldn't wait that long to hold the sale of America and he returned my deposit.

But it all went through much quicker than any of us expected and in early January, the contract on the house sale was signed and sealed. Most of the money was transferred to my offshore account. I drove to Perugia, paid the camper guy for America and for installing a solar panel on her roof. Ten days later, friends drove me to the dealership and I drove America back to what had been my home town and parked her across the road from the garbage bins.

19

Virgin Territory

Surprisingly, the town of Tuscania isn't in Tuscany. It's in northern Lazio, the same Italian region as Rome. The town is almost twenty kilometres or twelve miles due south of Lake Bolsena.

The old town of Tuscania is like a pearl hidden within the barnacle encrusted shell of the new metrolollipopolis that spreads out across the surrounding rolling olive tree estates crisscrossed by overhead pyloned power cables and bordered by tacky bill boards that jump out at you from behind the holm and cork oak trees that hide the hideously kitschy concrete country villas of the dirty newly laundered unwashed tax evaders that litter northern Lazio. The shell of Tuscania, the shabby concrete low-rise sprawl of factories, workshops, garages and housing complexes, hides a heart enclosed in an almost intact curtain medieval wall built with golden volcanic tufa stone.

Tufa can be cruel as well as kind. Spewed out from active volcanoes thousands of years ago, settled and cooled, it is a medium hard soft rock, somewhere half way between basalt and pumice. It has no strata and its middling density makes it easy to saw or hew into building blocks. It can be a glowing honey colour which brings a smile of surprise or recognition to the face of the unsuspecting newcomer or the hardened visitor to Orvieto in Umbria and Pitigliano in southern Tuscany, or it can be a pitilessly dull, depressing, dark grey, almost basalty black like in other towns in this part of central Italy that was once covered with the lava from the now extinct volcanic craters of the present lakes of Bolsena, Vico and Bracciano. A geologist once explained the chemo-geology of a volcanic eruption to me but in the end, whether your town was gifted with a golden glow or stuck in a greyish gloom was all down to a matter of chance, luck and prevailing winds.

Inside the medieval walls of Tuscania, the basalt cobbled streets are lined with elegant old town houses often with shops and workshops at street level. There are larger *palazzi*, public buildings and churches. The largest square in the town is decorated with the tops of Etruscan sarcophagi, the personalised coffin lids with the reclining figures of their one time occupants carved in *peporino*, another of the volcanic geological types of stone. The figures at street level have lost their heads to vandals and collectors. High on a wall on one side of the piazza, figures with their heads intact lounge in their relative safety and are often shrouded by the flowering trees in the garden of the deconsecrated church and the municipal library behind it.

If you walk through the gate to the right of the town hall, itself to the right of the wall, you leave the town's walls and head south towards a hill. On top of that hill sits the most beautiful Romanesque church in Europe.

San Pietro in Tuscania, also built from that golden tufa stone, is a tall *basilica* with a row of blind arcading crowning the exterior of the apse. Walking up to it are more headless Etruscan corpses frozen in stone and time, a small car park opposite a little gift and souvenir shop and a splendid fountain spurting one of the sweetest waters you'll find anywhere. To the right of the fountain a gateway leads into the church grounds. A random arch, a tall tower and remains of what were tall towers sit incongruously across from a long building, once the presbytery, now home to the caretakers and their families.

To the left of this building is the jewel, San Pietro, though your eye has already been drawn to the white marble carving on the facade of the nave the moment you came through the gate. Dragons and monsters swirl amid trailing vines and the angel, lion, eagle and bull of the apostles watch over the four cardinal points around the glorious rose window with two, small biform windows on either side.

The nave is lined by a colonnade of columns each with a different capital. The floor is one large ancient mosaic and the south aisle has Etruscan sarcophagi lids with reclining figures who've all managed to keep their heads. After a *baldacino*in white marble, the tent like canopy over the altar, a weird pulpit, more a rostrum in marble and brick, it's down some steps in the eastern aisle and into the darkness of the most exquisite crypt with a party of delicate columns of various dimensions of fragility actually holding up the series of dancing vaults that, in turn, seemed to be supporting everything up above and had been doing so for over seven hundred years. The crypt is almost Islamic. It's almost Alhambresque. In fact the whole feel of the place, the Etruscan bits, the cacophony of Doric, Ionic and Corinthian capitals, the mixture of pagan and Christian, the rough tufa in contrast to the smooth white marble, the raw wood of the beams supporting the truss roof, all create a melting pot of cultures, religions, materials and history.

Just to the right of the main altar on the instep of an arch is one of the few remaining pieces of fresco painting to have survived time, damp and earthquakes. It shows a Madonna della Misericordia, the Madonna of Mercy, the image of which Arezzo is so well endowed. The Virgin Mary stands holding out her cloak. Beneath its shelter kneel the little people. On the right hand side are the women, looking up to the great mother figure. Six of them with heads swaddled in scarves gaze up in awe. The seventh has her strawberry blonde hair tied in an ornate set of bands. She looks out just past our right shoulders with a knowing expression in her eyes.

The face of this lady is the spitting image of Astrid.

When you're up against a bullet-pocked wall and looking down the rifle barrels of the firing squad having foregone the optional blindfold, who do you call out to? Who do you ask for help? Superman ain't gonna swoosh down from a nearby skyscraper and sweep you to safety. This isn't a painting by Goya or Manet. This is you on trial in a foreign country in spite of the fact that you've lived in it for twenty years. Who do you turn to for help?

If you were up in front of a Sharia court and hoped you'd get off with beheading for your crime of adultery instead of being stoned to death, wouldn't you pray to the big A and his prophet? He's far more likely to get you off with a lighter sentence than Jesus, Krishna or Ngai. If you were one of the gunpowder plotters along with that guy that got caught and faced being hung drawn and quartered or beheaded, you wouldn't pray to the big Buddha would you?

You call on the local deities even if you're a dyed in the wool atheist as they're the ones that hold sway. They call the shots. They run the show.

In that court house in Perugia years ago I turned to the Madonna for company and comfort. Whether she actually helped I have not the slightest idea but she was the only person I thought I could talk to in a courthouse that, at first, seemed to be packed with a lynch mob. Even my lawyer in his uselessness seemed to be a plant by the prosecution.

Standing before the Madonna della Misericordia in San Pietro in Tuscania, the symbol of medieval justice as well as protectress against the plague as I knew from Arezzo, and looking at the strawberry blonde who must have had some special relationship with the painter - mistress, sister, daughter - I had an epiphany. I decided to see how many versions of her I could find, see and photograph before either I lost my court case, my house and my life, or managed to get out of Italy with what I could save. It would keep my mind off events in Perugia, and get me out more.

Being a convinced atheist, I had no qualms about Googling her. The search engine came up with over eighty pages on the Madonna della Misericordia. I checked, rechecked, again and again, and was sure there wasn't a single work or volume dealing with the subject; just more than two thousand disparate entries.

Helped by Massimo, who ran one of the two remaining internet points in Bolsena to survive Italy's recent draconian anti-terrorist laws, I drew up a list of Madonnas of Mercy beginning with the references to her closest to where I hoped I wouldn't have to live for very much longer. I was determined in the time remaining to me, to track down and see how many more of them I could find. I wanted to become the world record holding hunter of Madonnas of Mercy. It couldn't possibly be very difficult as I was sure there wasn't much competition.

I began to find them one by one, in little chapels in remote villages, parish churches tucked away under the Appenines, provincial museums dotted along the Tiber river valley. There they were hidden away. The churches were almost always locked so I had to write down the times of the mass and get there ten minutes before the service on the Sunday to ask the itinerant priests if I could photograph their Madonnas. They never refused. Mostly they took pride in showing me their treasured icons often going to great lengths to unlock gnarled wooden doors with giant rusty keys to let me into the sanctuaries. One priest, (after I made an appointment by phone,) set up a church committee reception for me with several elderly parishioners and the local historian, all standing around the painted wooden panel proud and curious about this foreigner interested in their heritage.

In one village chapel close to Lake Trasimeno, the cleaning lady talked me through the fresco behind the altar giving me vivid details of the spread of bubonic plague as it scythed its way through swathes of the population on its deadly harvest south westwards down the via Flaminia from Rimini to Rome in the mid fifteenth century.

This was the same village where that Greenpeace guy once lived. David McTaggart, the guy who sailed his yacht into the French Pacific nuclear testing zone and became a living legend. I met him a couple of times. The first time was in a bar in Cortona after one of my lectures. He was drinking aromatic herbal Sicilian killer liquors by the thimble-sized glassfuls with a couple of gay ladies I knew. He said he'd enjoyed my book 'Before the Palio' and called it "down to earth", which, from him, I took as a compliment. He went on and asked me if I wanted another story and did I know why the water level of Lake Trasimeno had dropped so drastically during the last decade?

"Irrigation. Irresponsible irrigation of cash crops

by greedy landowners sucking water from a massive, shallow puddle."

"Close" replied the living legend.

How can I be close? I thought. I knew I was spot on as I'd monitored the dropping water level of the lake as I led groups of kids onto the ferries to the treasure island. Years ago we used to walk *up* the ramp onto the ferries from the pier. Recently we walked *down.*

But he was a living legend so I held my tongue.

McTaggart said he had a massive dossier on the lake with lists of names of the landowners, their contacts within the municipal councils and proof of bribes taken. I said I couldn't possibly take up his offer as I was already out of my depth in legal hot water with the region of Umbria, but thanked him for the offer. Quietly I felt flattered that I'd been asked.

I saw him again during the following olive picking season. He had olive trees on his estate near the chapel with the Madonna where the cleaning lady was so informative. People who own olive trees always insist that their olive oil is the best in the world. When it's time for the harvest in early winter, they'll skip their grandmother's funeral if the weather is olive picking good time.

McTaggart was in a hurry as we briefly exchanged the time of year in Piazza Garribaldi. He was on his way back to pick his olives. The next I heard about him was that he was dead.

He'd been killed in a head-on car smash while driving back from lunch with one of the gay ladies I knew. I read about it in a newspaper and called her up. She said he hadn't been drinking as they'd lunched with a teetotaller. She was the last person to talk to him.

Not the last person or people to see him. They were a couple of elderly Italians toddling along in their Fiat Panda when this white Volkswagen Golf veered off the opposite lane and careened towards them with this moustachioed guy at the wheel an instant before the lights went out.

A heart attack was the official verdict after the autopsy. That's what they said after pope John Paul the first died after barely one month as spiritual leader of the Roman Catholic Church. This one-time village priest who'd risen through the ranks of the church in his native Veneto region in north east Italy had discovered gross financial irregularities within the papal banking system and his first stated objective when he was surprisingly elected pontiff was to get to the bottom of the matter. After thirty one nights in the papal apartment, he drank his last cup of coffee of the day brought to him by a caring nun, went to bed and never woke up in the morning. There were too many people who had too much to lose if he'd stayed on and carried out his declared aims and they all had access to his Holiness from within the walls of the Vatican itself. And why did John Paul the first's successor John Paul the second call himself John Paul? Was it so you'd remember pope John Paul by his papacy not his predecessors? Was it a cover up job?

There were the landowners and the municipal officials around Lake Trasimeno who had everything to lose if this living legend pursued his investigation into their ecologically disastrous misuse of a public asset. All it needed was a couple of nuts loosened and a small hacksaw job when that white Volkswagen Golf was being serviced and the living legend would live no more.

I went to his funeral on the triangle of green just outside the old village where the mayor, dignitaries, environmentalists from far and wide with family and friends had gathered. I stood next to the head of the Italian Green party, a certain aristocrat who'd recently written a newspaper article on the low level of the water in Lake Trasimeno. He wrote that short-sighted irresponsible irrigation using the lake's water was like chopping up an antique wooden heirloom, a piece of ancient furniture and burning it in a woodstove. It burnt really well and gave off a wonderful heat. I itched to ask him about McTaggart's concern about the water level of Lake Trasimeno and if there was any connection with that and his death but I chickened out as it seemed inappropriate on this occasion.

Boring funereal eulogies followed after far less than a minute's silence was called for in memory of the elderly couple in the Fiat Panda. But the present head of Greenpeace made up for things. His was the last speech and the one that was memorable. This is it as I recall:

"It was at the Children of Chernobyl budget meeting and things weren't going well. David was with the other leaders at the head table and he looked bored. The budget proposer droned on and on. In the welcome coffee break, David took me aside, handed me a T-shirt and told me to put it on under my pullover. He told me that back in the meeting, after a few minutes, I should take off my pullover. He was adamant he wanted the T-shirt back afterwards.

Well, with the coffee break over, everyone ambled back into the meeting hall and after about five minutes into the budget lady's speech, I took off my pullover. Across the front of the T-shirt was screen printed

PERSONALLY I BLAME McTAGGART

Someone in the meeting laughed. Then another. Quickly more. Then the whole meeting cracked up and rocked with laughter. The budget was passed, the meeting ended and that was David McTaggart. And personally I DO blame McTaggart. I blame him for putting an end to French nuclear testing in the Pacific. I blame him for stopping Norwegian whaling. Now we have no one to blame!"

Great speech. I was about to ask the cleaning lady if she knew what an exceptional man had lived near her village when she said she had to close the chapel and go home as she had to meet her kids off the school bus. I drove home too and a couple of weeks later received a registered letter from the town hall of the village where I'd photographed their Madonna of Mercy, listened to the erudite cleaning lady and attended the funeral of their illustrious foreigner, the dead legend. The letter contained a speeding ticket.

Museums were far less co-operative when it came to photographing Madonnas of Mercy, with the exception of Arezzo.

Taking photographs using a flash in museums in Italy is almost always strictly forbidden, I think only so you'll have to buy their postcards instead.

In the Bargello museum in Florence I was in luck as the curator in the room with the painted wooden Madonna and her tiny refugees was asleep. Snooty Siena weren't having any of my research excuses. According to my internet sources, in the former hospital of Saint Mary of the Staircase across from the cathedral whose frescoed walls and ceilings had been restored, there were two. I met a man years ago who'd been admitted to the hospital with acute appendicitis. When he came round from the anaesthetic, the first things he saw were the rich decorations on the ceiling and he thought he'd died and gone to heaven. As a museum they were playing by the rules. The helpful lady serving in the shop showed me the Madonna. The chunk of fresco with her head was missing but the little people were all there. The shop lady asked permission from her boss. I heard the clear "Non" from outside the office so I set my camera focused on the correct distance. The Madonna was conveniently close to the exit. Before the custodians realised, there was a flash. I had the photo and was out into the sunshine before you could say Aldo Rossi.

The most famous of all the Madonnas of Mercy has to be that by Piero della Francesca in San Sepolchro in the eastern tip of Tuscany. No way was I going to be able to photograph her. The lady custodian tailed me from the moment I entered the museum like she knew what I was up to. I had to make do with a postcard.

The Medieval and Modern museum in Arezzo couldn't have been more helpful. I'd made an appointment through the official channels and on the day met a lady who introduced herself as Jane, an unusual name for an Italian lady. She took me round the museum which I knew by heart and photographed the six Madonnas. I was packing up my equipment when she asked me if I didn't want to see the seventh upstairs. I didn't know it existed. After I'd photographed it I took her for a coffee in a bar outside and when I left I forgot my tripod in the bar. I was so not used to using one in my Madonna hunting expeditions.

When I had about twenty five Madonnas photographed and documented, I went back to San Pietro in Tuscania for another refresher. There she was that strawberry blonde, not run of the mill, not one of the sheep, an exception to the rule, looking off to one side.

The Madonna herself, was holding out her protective cloak, staring out into the distance, vacuously. They all seem to, all the ones I've seen anyway. I guess if you've been stuck there with your arms outstretched for all those years, it does get a bit tiring and tedious. She's probably got varicose veins with all that standing, poor dear. But under her cloak is where the action is. That's where it's all happening. Strawberry blondes for ever.

I asked the caretaker on the door of San Pietro in Tuscania if he knows who painted the fresco. He said he didn't but he knew who probably did and he wrote a name onto a piece of paper.

Signor Ellio Stacinni,
Biblioteca municipale, Tuscania

I thanked him and went into the town. The public library was behind the wall lined with the lounging stone Etruscans. I went up the steps and round the church. The library was closed.

On another weekday I returned and the library was open. I asked the young man at the desk for Signor Ellio Stacinni and was told he was downstairs and I should knock first. At the bottom of the stairs I knocked on the large wooden door and a voice replied

"Venite."

Inside was a large vaulted tufo ceiling with patches of fresco. The sunlit room was lined with bookshelves. In one part was a long wooden table and sitting at one end were two elderly gentlemen either side of the man sitting at the head of the table.

"Signor Ellio Stacinni?"

"*Sono io.*" said the man at the head of the table getting up from his chair. He was tall and well built and had a completely bald head. He was dressed in smart casual baggy brown trousers and an open necked striped shirt. He smiled and reached out and shook my hand.

"I've come to ask you some questions about the Madonna della Misericordia" I said.

All three men burst out laughing. Seeing I looked puzzled, Signor Ellio said

"We were just talking about her. Can you come back later?"

"How much later?" I asked.

"Half an hour."

For one moment I thought he was going to say

next week so I thanked him and left them to chew that one over.

I went to the bar in the piazza below the Etruscan layabouts and had a cappuccino. Signor Stacinni reminded me of someone but I couldn't put my finger on the face. As the half hour was up, I paid and went across, through the gate and up the steps. At the top it hit me. The Judge! In Cormack McCarthy's 'Blood Meridian'! He fitted perfectly but no way was a librarian in a small provincial town in Italy going to be a character like that larger than life enigmatic genius of a monster. It was just his appearance.

He was alone when I knocked again. He offered me a seat at the table and I sat down and told him what I'd been up to these last weeks and handed him my camera so he could see the pictures himself. He was obviously deeply interested as he examined each one intently. When he got to the last one which was the first I'd taken, his eyes lit up even more.

"She's our local lady, or one of them" he said.

"That's where I started, with her."

He stood up and asked me to follow him to the far side of the room where there was a large paper-strewn desk and offered me a chair beside it. He rummaged through the papers and drew out a sheet and handed it to me. It had a list of titles, dates and locations and was headed Madonna della Misericordia.

"There's nothing on her. There's no overall tome" he said.

"That's what I found out too" I replied.

"I've written a book about the local Madonna in San Pietro, a novel. It's actually about one of the ladies sheltering under her cloak." He took out a photograph of the fresco and pointed to the top lady, the strawberry blonde with the fancy hairdo.

I didn't tell him that she'd got me going too, as she reminded me very much of someone I'd known some years ago who seemed to weave in and out of my life.

We went through his list and compared notes. He had some I didn't, and I had some not on his list.

I explained I was planning to leave Italy soon. I didn't know exactly when and I didn't explain why. We agreed we'd compile as comprehensive a database on the subject as possible and we exchanged phone numbers.

For my last few weeks in Italy I used the good excuse of hunting Madonnas of Mercy to visit places I'd never seen before and to return to old haunts.

Turning off the via Flaminia, the Roman road from Rimini to the Eternal City, not far from where the remains of the bridge of Augustus built two thousand years ago stand, and winding down a dirt track through farms and smart country houses, I eventually found the charming and beautifully restored tiny Romanesque church of Santa Pudenziana. It was a church popular for weddings which is how I got in by calling the number posted on the door. On the afternoon of my appointment small groups of people gathered in the area in front of the church. As we waited for the guardian to arrive I had a look at the farm just below. Parked outside a hay barn was a white, state-of-the-art, Mercedes Benz 500 convertible coupé! Some farmers. The lady with the keys arrived, unlocked the heavy wooden door and let us in. A young couple immediately got into an animated conversation with her obviously planning their wedding. A group of Germans nosied around while I photographed the Madonna who was frescoed low down on the side of the narrow nave. She was very primitive compared to some I'd seen and the figures under her cloak looked like dolls lined up in a children's toy shop. In its own intimate way the church was a San Pietro in Tuscania in miniature right down to the crypt.

Eventually I even made it to Rieti, a town whose motto was "The centre of Italy in the middle of nowhere." Rieti was the destination of the via Salaria from Rome, the road up which salt was transported. Every schoolboy knows that Roman legionnaires were once paid in salt, hence salary. The town is on a plain, surrounded by towering Appenine mountains. The day I went they were capped in snow and sleet made driving difficult. The church where there was a Madonna I wanted to see was closed so I went home and didn't go back to Rieti. Nothing there.

The last group of Madonnas I had to see, where there were more of them than in any one city other than Arezzo, was in Venice.

20

Divorce in Venice

As I had planned my flight from Italy to avoid losing all I had to a miserable, misogynist, money-grabbing, misfit, I needed to see and record the Madonnas of Mercy in Venice. It was a good enough way of saying goodbye.

I took a train like I'd done years before on my way to get divorced, though that wasn't on my itinerary. I was taking my then four-year-old daughter who'd spent the summer with me, back to her mother who was staying in Venice.

I'd packed a picnic lunch for us as it was a journey of several hours. I included a Kinder egg for her, one of those hollow chocolate eggs containing a yellow plastic eggish shaped container which held a *sorpressa*, a surprise, usually a miniature multi-coloured ready-to-assemble plastic aeroplane car or whatever. The yellow containers are two tightly fitted halves and the easiest way to open them is to put them in your mouth and bite them. They pop open and you catch the surprise. My daughter usually gave me the job of biting open the yellow egg.

During long train journeys we had a repertoire of amusements: I spy which was good for about half an hour. Drawing, good for hours, reading stories and playing house which was only possible when the compartment was relatively empty. On that journey, occupying the compartment with us were an older man and a teenage boy, both Italian, probably father and son, who sat in the opposite corner by the outside window. For almost the whole journey they took not the slightest bit of notice of us, being totally absorbed in their conversations. We just played our games.

After Bologna it was lunchtime and I unpacked the sandwiches. The two Italians looked up and paused in their chatter. Food! My daughter munched her way through her *pannini* and mouthful after mouthful was closely observed by our neighbours. Finally it came to the Kinder egg and its hidden treat. She carefully unwrapped the chocolate, folded the coloured metallic paper and put it in her little hand case. She bit into the chocolate and caught the pieces as they broke and began to savour the rich flavour. About halfway through, she extracted the inner yellow egg and handed it to me for the treatment. The Italians were riveted. As I put the plastic egg into my mouth both father and son leapt up in horror and cried:

"Questo non si mangia!" You don't eat that!

We arrived hours before I was due to hand her

over so I took my daughter on a tour by waterbus, the famous *vaporetto*.

It was Josephine who'd explained to me how to get around Venice back when I was working for the British Council. They don't make grand English ladies like Josephine any longer - alas. Maybe the world was only big enough for one of her at a time and now that the earth has shrunk, there probably isn't room for even one like her any more.

She met me at the British pavilion, a former tea-house in what were the Napoleonic gardens, now the home of the Venice Biennale. Josephine's ample late middle-aged frame was dressed in a billowing summer frock and her eyes sparkled from under her broad brimmed straw hat as carried me off to lunch like booty. She took me on the cheapest gondola ride in Venice, a ferry that still crosses the Grand Canal by the Accademia bridge.

"You have to go on a gondola at least once my boy and there's no point in throwing money at the experience."

She boomed this advice as we disembarked and she tacked down a *cali*, one of the narrow streets alongside a glittering smelly canal, avoiding the skinny cats, weaving from left to right in full sail, chucking an old man under the chin here, greeting a friend there, receiving bows and graces left and right until we arrived at her chosen watering spot, what appeared to a novice to be a fish market stall but was a display of mostly live sea food to choose from at the entrance to a restaurant inside. Our selection would be cooked as we willed and brought to our table. I let Josephine do the choosing and the ordering as waiters scrambled to kiss her hand, pull back her chair and generally run around her every whim, fussing and carrying on about her. You could tell she loved every moment of it along with the food and the wine.

During the long drawn out meal she gave me a potted history of the Serene Republic, the Biennale and my role in it, a lesson on Italian manners, customs and behaviour, where to eat out well for next to nothing, what sights were not to be missed, what was missable, and tips for getting around easily on the water transport system. She also leaked out details of her life: she'd married a Venetian, swept off her feet barely out of school, settled down but never had children. ("A lucky thing for them, poor never-had-beens.") Her husband died leaving her high, dry and fairly well off in an apartment on the Guidecca when she met the Dame of the British Empire, Lillian Sommerville, my then boss, who was looking for a caretaker for her pavilion at the Biennale, someone on the spot. That was in the fifties and she'd stuck with it along with a bit of English teaching and the odd translation or guided tour. Then in her sixties going on some, she was part of the Venetian glass work, a larger than life piece of the overall mosaic. That was the first of several lunches we spent together. It felt like being taken out by a great aunt and there never seemed to be a bill presented at the end of any of those meals with Josephine.

I took my daughter through Saint Marc's square to see the pigeons and she squealed with delight as they pecked at the maize seeds she held out for them.

Back when I'd met Josephine, Giorgio the owner of the pensione Orion where I was staying, invited me to watch the World Cup soccer final on his black and white TV in the lobby. Italy were playing Brazil. A quarter of an hour into the match the phone rang. He picked up the receiver, listened puzzled then passed it to me. An obviously Australian lady had landed at Piazza San Marco and wanted to be led to the pensione where she had a room booked. Giorgio pleaded with me to go as watching every second of the match was so important to him, so I went down the cali and crossed Piazza San Marco which was almost completely empty and silent except for a few bewildered tourists wondering where the waiters and musicians had gone. Suddenly, from nowhere and everywhere, cheering erupted in quadrophonia. Italy had scored! I met the lady and guided her back to the pensione where a dejected Giorgio told me Brazil had retaliated. It was one all. Brazil eventually went on to win four goals to one. Giorgio was devastated. He went into mourning for the whole of the next day.

When we'd run out of pigeon feed and my daughter posed for one last tourist photo, I took her back on the vaporetto to the railway station. Her mother was waiting and as I kissed goodbye and handed over my tearful little girl, her mother handed me a thick white envelope.

On the train home I opened it. It contained legal papers, and that was my Venetian divorce. Cheap, quick and easy.

Now I was tracking down the last Madonnas of Mercy for my collection and I left Venice Santa Lucia railway station, bought a ticket and waited by the Grand Canal for the number 1 *vaporetto.* Venice was basking in an Indian summer. I'd seen it much more crowded and there was room at the bow end when the water bus arrived. This is the best way to see the Grand Canal, from the bow of the No 1, but this time I wasn't going that far and I joined a small group who got off at San Marcuola.

Alongside a small canal I found the Scuola Vecchia della Misericordia that still contained the traces of where the relief said to be in the Victoria and Albert museum in London had been. In my guide book I noticed a tiny photo with a subtext recommending the archway to the Corta Nova. I'd walked right past it. I walked back and found her over the entrance and took several photos with the sun shining directly onto the white marble of the statue of the Virgin sheltering the little people under her cloak. There's another one over what's called the Arch of Paradise but there was no time to hunt her down without any idea where to start.

It was hot and I started sweating so removed my jacket, took off my pullover and put on my jacket again and walked back towards the Grand Canal and went into the shop I'd seen earlier selling what looked to be Italian fish and chips. I bought and ate a delicious anchovy filled batter cake and caught the next No1 water bus to San Tomà, two stops after the Rialto bridge, which was packed as usual. Piazza San Tomà was busy too. I found the building I wanted, the Scuola dei Calegheri, once the guild of shoemakers. The sun was still shining on the relief of the Madonna on the brick facade. Tourists sitting at a restaurant table looked up to what I was photographing as if there was something they'd missed. When they saw a statue of a lady with a few people kneeling beside her they turned back to their meal. I walked back to the Rialto bridge and wound my way to San Giovanni and Paolo where I'd taken a group of American students to see a vase containing the skin of Marcantonio Brigadin. He was the Venetian commander of Famagusta in the 16th century and was captured by the besieging moors, had his nose cut off, was dragged around the walls of the city, hung from the mast of a galley then skinned alive. His skin was later recaptured by the Venetians and enshrined in an urn in the church. I'd told the students the story and that there was nothing to see but the urn but their appetite for gore was aroused and surprisingly they stood in the gloom of the church looking up at this vase in awed silence far beyond their normal attention span.

I found Santa Maria Formose nearby, was surprised to have to pay to go in but I saw what I was after, across the nave. An American father and his small daughter turned away when they were asked to pay. I almost said there was a painting in this church that was well worth the entrance fee but suddenly saw myself as a tousled geek trainspotting Madonnas with a mad gleam in his eye and thought the better of it. Just as well. I photographed the Madonna painted by Vivarini in 1474 looking in as good a condition today as if it were painted yesterday, in her ornate fake marble setting of pilasters and niches.

Outside in the piazza I sat at the bar and ordered a

Scottish beer and half a hot dog from a waitress who gave me strange looks. After a second beer I trolled slowly back to Santa Lucia, stopping at an Irish bar for Guinnesses, with Manchester United soccer live on TV. I planned to go to Mantua to see the frescoes by Mantegna in the Palazzo Gonzaga. The train left punctually. I sat on a double seat with an empty seat opposite. The ticket collector gave me a sideways look as he checked I wasn't trying to cheat the state railway. At a station others got on board. A woman approached the vacant seats opposite me, then obviously changed her mind and sat somewhere else.

It was dark when I got to Mantova. I needed to find a hotel. There was a street of them and I tried each one but they were all full, though, I couldn't see many guests milling about in any of them. I was hungry and settled on a fast pizza place. I ordered a four seasons and the lady gave me a 'we've seen all sorts in here' look and served me my order. I sat down at a stool against a bench with a large mirrored wall. As I munched my pizza I saw my reflection in the mirror. I'd not put my jacket on properly and it was all jumbled up behind me. I looked like a tramp, a real bum who'd just been pulled out from a bar room brawl by his legs. No wonder the hotels were full. I straightened myself out, finished my pizza, walked back to the station and took a train to Bologna. The ticket office there showed a 1.30 am train that stopped in Florence and Orvieto. It was perfect. I bought a ticket and walked up into the town which was humming. There were crowds of people walking about in couples and groups under the city's famous arcades. I walked under the tallest medieval tower in Italy that I'd climbed thirty three years ago and looked down over its leaning neighbour. I sat at a bar and drank beers until an hour after midnight. The town looked like it still had plenty of partying to do but I got on my train, squeezed into a seat in an almost full compartment. The train was going to Naples and only had four carriages. It felt like a ghost train but it dropped me off in Orvieto at 4.00 precisely.

I drove home and sat up until dawn checking through all my photographs with the help of a bottle of wine. I wondered what I was doing, a non-academic dyed in the wool atheist, still, after eight years, up to his neck in legal shit creek without a paddle, going to all these out of the way places photographing Madonnas of Mercy? I had possibly the biggest collection in the world and I had no idea what I was going to do with them all.

I poured myself another glass of wine, then as the sun came up, an idea came through the window with the light.

21

On the road

Professor Carlo Ginsberg, when professor of history at the University of Bologna, wrote a book called 'The Enigma of Piero', the first book in Italian I ever read from front to back.

Without going into the details, it was clear from the book that Professor Ginsberg was an academic who could and would transcend academic boundaries, bringing an astute historical eye into the world of art history, shedding new light on Piero della Francesca's paintings, especially the identities of some of the characters he portrayed. Piero had painted a Madonna of Mercy too so there was a link to what I had in mind.

I was used to British academia with some professors like my supervisor at the university where I took a masters degree in art history.

"My landlady just committed suicide and my mother died yesterday. I need time off." I told him.

"But what about my essays?" was the sympathetic response I got.

I tried again. "My landlady just killed herself because she couldn't face another Christmas without seeing her grandchildren as her son thought she was going mad. My mother just died because she was scared shitless of dying of cancer and that's what she died of. You should have seen her expression when she woke up after an operation to remove a lump and they'd chopped off her tits."

"But I need your essays to grade your work."

I should have spat in his face. I managed to spend all my time there not showing up at any of his little soirees for us post-graduate students.

That university denied me my masters piece of paper because I owed fifty pennies for a lost room key. I told them if that was all their post-graduate degrees were worth they could stuff it up their creative writing hole. Months later I went back to the university as my then wife was still attending. In the secretary's office a lady behind the desk handed me my post-graduate degree certificate saying it had been sitting there for ages.

I decided I would take my fat Madonna of Mercy file to Professor Ginsberg who had moved to the University of Pisa. Hopefully, he would pass it on to one of his students as it shouldn't be left in mid air. It was half a PhD sitting on a plate. The plan was convenient too. I wanted to drive America out of Italy via Pisa as I wanted to say goodbye to someone extra special. All goodbyes are special and I die a little each time I say another.

When Michelangela won against the plaintiff's appeal, the injunction on my house was lifted and the sale went through. I moved most of the money into an offshore account, collected the log book of the camper from the dealers below Perugia, paid Michelangela in cash (which she'd hidden among the dried flowers in the bowl on her desk in her office) before I took her out to a thank you and goodbye lunch of oysters and other seafood in a restaurant beside lake Trasimeno. I'd been taken out to a goodbye lunch the day before near the ancient forum in Rome by Donatella, the notary who'd overseen all the ups and downs of my Italian life for the last thirty three years. We too had oysters and other seafood. I'd taken Ellie to Tacconi's trattoria in Cortona for a last meal together to say farewell and that I was sure we'd meet up again. Finally, fish again, lake fish this time at Picchietto's family restaurant in Bolsena, with my pals who'd helped me empty out the old house and get rid of most of my possessions. I'd paid almost all my bills except the one at the oldest bank in Italy who said I couldn't close my account. As they were the oldest bank in Italy I figured they could survive a bit longer without being paid. I'd wiped the slate as clean as possible. I was ready to go.

America was packed up with my greatly reduced possessions which was like having a weight off my shoulders. I'd reduced my baggage down to essential clothes, basic kitchen utensils, only the books I really would read again, my photographs and letters, camera, laptop, a wooden painted statuette of Ruggiero on horseback killing a dragon who was about to rape Angelica before eating her, and a 16th century terracotta head of a lady with a convoluted hairdo that I'd rescued from beneath some steps leading up to a villa in Arezzo. We were all rolling along on four pieces of air-filled rubber.

America is heavy and solidly built. I'd stowed everything carefully so stuff wouldn't fall about on the curves. We hit the series of hairpin bends that climb up onto the plateau of the lava flow and got one last look back at the dear old city of Orvieto, which had been home for many years. On sunny evenings depending on the time of year, this is the place where the setting sun hits the mosaics on the triple triangle pinnacles of the west facade of the cathedral and splashes gold across the valley. We rounded a corner and I closed a door on a big chapter.

The engine was big but I had to change down again and again on the hills and rapidly gathered a trail of following vehicles. I drove down to lake Bolsena, my home for the last four years and the umbilical belly button of ancient Italy. This is where the last of the Etruscans, the Volsinii were exiled beside the largest volcanic lake in Europe.

I didn't stop this time. I wasn't sad to be leaving Bolsena. Relieved really. I'd felt trapped there these last two years. What was really a pretty little town had become a prison of my own making. Besides, the elderly neighbour who owned the olive grove I overlooked from the terrace had died and her nephew'd moved in with his nasty barking dogs and the council was going to move the garbage containers to right outside my front door. The rats weren't far behind. But just in time I'd been able to break free and escape. See ya folks.

America trundled along the old Via Francigana, once the pilgrim route to Rome, up the hill past the perfectly maintained war cemetery where the oldest soldier was twenty eight when he died about the time I had my first birthday. The road from Montefiascone to Marta is one long tree lined avenue. Someday an idiot son of some town councillor will crash his speeding car against one and kill himself and they'll cut all the trees down as a danger to drivers.

One last lunch at Gino's restaurant in Martha, the best in the area. Gino didn't believe I was leaving Italy. His eels cooked in white wine are the best. He tried to get me drunk on his *acqua del lago*, a potent turquoise liquor but nothing was going to stop me now. I said goodbyes and staggered to America and cast off. Way over the limit, I let America drive on automatic pilot. We passed through Tuscania and I waved to Ennio and the lady under the cloak in the church on the hill. I had to see two other ladies on my way to Spain. One I'd known all her life. The other I'd never met, although I knew an awful lot about her.

Orbetello sits on the middle of three promontories that converge on Monte Argentario, a sort of chunky island about five kilometres off the mainland shore of Italy and looks like a it's being pulled away from the Tuscan coast into the Tyrrhenian sea like a piece of cheese covered bread from a Swiss fondue, leaving trailers of stretchy strings of melted cheese in its wake.

Orbetello sits in about the centre of the middle of the three strings of hot Emmenthal.

Porto Santo Stefano and Port'Ercole on Monte Argentario itself are overpriced tourist traps for yachty people who aren't half as smart as they imagine. Even in winter the two ports charge exorbitant prices for average meals with half a view of rough sea.

Orbetello is Tuscany's best kept seaside secret. It's where Italians go in July and August. Foreigners are thin on the ground. I discovered it with my daughter one September after we'd searched in vain for a reasonably priced hotel room in both of the ports. We gave up on them and drove into Orbetello and found the Pensione Piccolo Parigi. It was perfect. We had a delicious sea food dinner in a tiny trattoria set back off the main street. The next day we took the ferry from Porto Santo Stefano to the island of Giglio which is the only good reason to go to Porto Santo Stefano. It was to Isola di Giglio where I planned to spend one last Sunday in Italy.

I parked America on some waste ground as there wasn't a campsite in the town and then went to the little trattoria I knew and had their version of fish soup, a *bouillabaisse* which is unique in that they cook *porcini* mushrooms with it.

The next morning I steered America across the promontory and drove round the coast road to Porto Santo Stefano and found a free parking place. At the harbour I bought a return ticket for the ferry to Giglio.

The ferry was nearly empty and the island was hidden in mist. It takes about an hour to get to Giglio and as we approached, the form of the island loomed out of the mist and the ferry eased into Porto.

Porto is a magical little harbour. It can't be more than five hundred metres from one end to the other. There are two sturdy stone barriers that reach out into the sea and shelter a variety of leisure craft, local fishing boats, the odd Police motor launch, all dwarfed by the ferries from the mainland. Along the harbour front are bars, restaurants and souvenir stalls. Some restaurants have outside annexes on the sea side. You can drink ice cold *limoncello* in frozen glasses or pig out on grilled prawns as people and boats come and go.

It was empty that February Sunday morning. The mist had cleared and the sun shone sharply on the white painted houses. I wandered aimlessly for about an hour. Tanned and weathered seamen hung around bars with their smiles and wrinkles, happy people. I found a sort of eating place and sat outside in the sun sheltered from the wind by the overhanging roof. I ordered spaghetti with a spicy tomato sauce and a bottle of red wine. The wine arrived with a plastic cup and the pasta arrived on a plastic plate and I ate it with plastic knife and fork. It was one of the best meals ever! The spaghetti was cooked perfectly to that point between *al* and *dente,* and the sauce had the sharp volcanic peppery smoothness that you only get down south. The wine was soft and rich. I went to the kitchen to compliment the cook and the waitress said it was her Napolitana mama! *Sola una Napolitana!*

I took the four-o'clock ferry back, slept off two post prandial *limoncellos en voyage* and woke as we entered Porto Santo Stefano. The sun was setting. I felt wide awake now and decided not to go back to Orbetello but keep going, so I drove America out onto the dual carriageway from Rome, the via Aurelia, and headed north for Pisa.

I called Lucy in Pisa. Lucy was my second daughter, almost. She and my daughter had grown up together since babies and had stayed the best of friends all their lives. Lucy is tall, slim with long blonde hair, blue eyes and a captivating smile. She worked for a holiday company called 'The Magic of Italy' and would greet holiday makers at Pisa airport with "Hello. I'm Lucy from Magic" which must have been the warmest greeting they ever met.

I'd known her mum and dad at art school. It was Lucy's mum a quarter of a century ago who told me that my ex-wife's new husband, when their recent marriage ran aground, should leave his new wife alone and trust his luck and I'd passed on the advice. I'd last seen Lucy's mum a year ago, the first time I'd been back in London after ten years. I was staying with my daughter, and one Saturday she said Lucy and her mum were coming round to visit and we all went to the local pub and had a wonderfully nostalgic couple of hours together with lots of laughter and photos. My daughter left for Paris on business the following Monday morning. On Tuesday evening she called to say Lucy's mum had died the night before - a brain haemorrhage - just like that. I was devastated as were all her family and friends, yet I felt privileged to have been in London and spent those couple of hours with her.

Just outside Pisa I called Lucy again and she talked me into Pisa on her moby, right up to a parking space next to another camper, close to her apartment. It was pissing with rain. We went out for a Chinese meal and the next day she showed me where the University of Pisa was, La Scuola Normale, seat of Professor Carlo Ginsberg.

It's an impressive high Renaissance palazzo off a piazza surrounded by similar majestic buildings with their decorated facades. A statue of their patron, Cosimo di Medici, basked in bronze out in the wintry sunshine. Inside the faculty I was shown to Professor Ginsberg's office where one of the secretaries told me he would be in the next day at three in the afternoon.

That night, asleep in America as the rain beat down on the roof, I had a dream: I was in a classroom sitting at a desk. There was only one other person in the classroom sitting at a desk against the far wall. He had reddish hair and wore a beige jacket. He was looking to the blackboard in front where, written in blue paint, was "Write a paper on ..." then a squiggle of blue paint. Not much of a dream but I remembered it clearly the next morning and told Lucy.

Minutes before three that afternoon I crossed the piazza, climbed the marble steps to the entrance to the university building. As I reached the ornately carved stone doorway, a bell somewhere rang out three times. The doors to the building opened and out walked four young men, students I guessed, and an older man with reddish hair wearing a beige jacket. I recognised him immediately as the man in the classroom in my dream. They went down the steps, crossed the piazza and disappeared. Inside the building I asked at the reception desk if I could see Professor Ginsberg and the lady said he'd just this minute left the building.

For some reason I didn't chase after him. After an afternoon of last minute Italian shopping, back at Lucy's place I wrapped up my Madonna file in plastic, then brown wrapping paper with a covering letter to Donatella in Rome. If I didn't get the file to Professor Ginsberg, she said she knew a professor at the Sapienza, one of two universities in Rome, who would be very interested in it.

The next morning I kissed Lucy goodbye, drove America to a post office and mailed the package to Donatella in Rome then hit the via Aurelia north bound along the coast of the Tyrrhenian Sea. It was still pissing with rain.

22
Pasta to tapas

Valentine's Day! That's as good a day as any to leave Italy - with love. I've known people who quit the Belle Paese with bitterness, even anger; baffled by their misunderstanding of the beautiful country's sometimes labyrinthine, Byzantine intricacies. Italy was good to me and, I hoped, I'd been good to Italy.

Last night I'd parked America on the sea front in San Remo, a lovely riviera resort town close to the French border, unjustly famous for its annual song festival. I found a parking space right on the sea front and hoped the traffic police wouldn't move me on but it was pissing down so hard they were probably staying indoors. In the old town I found one of those old-time hardware stores, a *ferramenta,* with a vast wooden chest of drawers almost as high as the ceiling with dozens of worn wooden drawers with a sample of each's content fixed to the outer face. It looked like it was run by three generations, *nonno, figlio é nipote,* all standing in identical blue overalls behind the counter serving a queue of customers. I'd seen a small gas lamp in the window and asked for it *per favore* and the one I took to be the grandson brought one to the counter, assembled it with clear instructions as he went. I bought a couple of extra gas cans and took them back to America then went out into the rainy night. In an almost empty restaurant I had fish soup. I was hoping for one last memorable meal but it didn't happen. The spaghetti on Giglio island was my last great Italian meal, eclipsed by the lunch with Donatella three days earlier. Lucy and I had had eaten Chinese my first night and she'd cooked dinner last night.

Back in America I lit my new gas lamp as the rain beat down on the roof. It was snug and cosy. In my bed over the driving cabin I opened the side window and heard the waves breaking on the beach.

Now I'm on my way to Avignon. I've got a date with a lady *sur le pont* or quite close by. America and I pass signposts that lead back to the towns of my childhood: Menton, Nice, Cannes, Le Cannet and especially Mandelieu.

At the beginning of the 1950's, when my mother was convinced by my godmother to leave Britain for Kenya, my younger brother and I went to France with our au pair Raimonde, while my sister stayed with my mother back in England until our house was sold.

Raimonde's family lived in a then tiny village called Mandelieu. In the midst of mimosa trees, olive groves and vineyards, there were a few dozen houses surrounding the dusty oval of the Place Jeanne d'Arc where the old men played *pétanque.* We went to the village school; collected the milk, still warm from the cow at the dairy farm; bread from the bakery where an old blind lady dressed in black sat gazing out through her eyeless sockets as she sorted seeds; trod grapes in the cellar below the house and went to midnight mass on Christmas eve. Raimonde's parents spoilt us boys silly. I was allowed to stoke the wood burning cooker until the kitchen became unbearably hot even for Raimonde's mother Madame Moulaire. Monsieur Moulaire, wearing his beret, would drive us little boys to the shops in Cannes singing "Jingle bells, jingle bells, stick peanuts up your arse".

Eventually my mother and sister arrived and we moved to the Moulaires' little house in Le Cannet, a suburb of Cannes and things were never the quite same.

As we drive past the sign for Mandelieu I'm tempted to try and find the Moulaires' house again. Over thirty years ago, as my wife and our almost two-year-old daughter drove to Italy in our battered old Mercedes Benz, I decided to call into the village which I hadn't seen for twenty five years.

Most people always advise never to go back to visit paradise as it will inevitably have been ruined especially if it was anywhere along the French riviera. I'd built up a mental picture of the little French village buried in concrete high-rises surrounded by tarmac and superhighways. I reminded myself of this bleak picture as we got close.

The sign for Mandelieu suddenly appeared and

we swerved off the *autoroute* and drove straight into .... concrete high-rises! Nothing looked familiar as we wandered through streets lined with supermarkets, bars, cafés, hardware stores, laundrettes, the usual high street collection.

"It's gone." I said to my wife, "The village doesn't exist any more."

Just as I was giving up hope, we rounded a corner and there it was! Place Jeanne d'Arc! Entirely intact but every conceivable square metre of flat surface had been tarmaced over and there were cars parked everywhere. There was the building which was once the school. That was where the bicycle repair shop had been. The dusty *pétanque* rink had been tarred over too and now sported a coloured metal children's climbing frame, a slide and a merry-go-round. The small shrubs I remembered had grown into sizable trees. We circled the square, as I remembered the house lay at the top of a street on the far side. We drove up what I thought was the right one and there, at the end stood the house, tiny now, but unmistakable. I was excited and parked the car. Leaving my wife and child inside, I opened the gate, walked up the flagstoned path to the front door not knowing what to expect and rang the doorbell. A few seconds later it was opened and there stood a thin elderly man with a pencil moustache and a black beret. Monsieur Moulaire!

"Bonjour Monsieur Moulaire. Je suis Martin. Est-ce que vous me reconnaissez?"

His face broke into that broad smile I remembered and he shook my hand warmly. He hadn't changed much! He looked exactly the same as when we waved goodbye to him, his wife and daughter on the railway station in Cannes as we set off for Marseilles, for Genoa, for Africa, almost twenty five years before.

"Et Madame Moulaire?" I asked.

He looked sad.

"Elle est morte il-y-a douze ans."

"I'm sorry" I said in English as I couldn't remember the condolence in French. He came outside and I introduced him to my wife and child and he invited us in for a drink saying he'd phone Raimonde in Cannes immediately. I explored the house: it was just as I'd left it down to the woodburning cooker in the kitchen only everywhere looked much smaller. I spoke to Raimonde who was at work and couldn't get back until the evening but she invited us for dinner. We didn't stay much longer as the language barrier re-asserted itself so we said *"A ce soir"* to Monsieur Moulaire and took off for the beach. Around six, we returned to Mendelieu.

Raimonde didn't look as I remembered her but was still Raimonde, who years ago cried with homesickness as she sat in our English parlour, fresh from France. She taught us French, played our games and taught us new ones, accompanied us to school and warned off the bullies, participated as we filled our bicycle pumps with water and squirted them into the keyhole of the neighbour's front door having rung the doorbell first. She described black people who for us, only existed in our 'Babar the Elephant' books and wiped our bums when we'd finished doing big jobs.

That summer evening, we five sat in the garden

and ate dinner and talked about the deaths of our mothers, the years in Africa, what the rest of our families were up to, who'd married and who hadn't. I told her we were on our way to live on a farm in Italy and she said she could never live in the city; she would only work there. She loved living here in the country. I looked up and there above us hung the idle jib of a crane on a new high-rise apartment block being completed across the road. The mimosa and olive trees had gone, and instead there were dense housing estates that stretched up the hill where I'd once hidden in the woods from the angry villagers after interfering with their game of *pétanque*. Suddenly I realised: they were blind to it! They didn't see the concrete and tarmac. This old man and his daughter saw the quiet dusty village as I remembered it. I wasn't disappointed at how almost everything had changed but they were both who they were and, thinking the worst, I'd imagined it exactly how it turned out to be.

Then it was time to go. We planned to drive through the night taking the intestinal coastal route through Nice, Monte Carlo and into Italy. We'd stop off at some promising resort on the Ligurian riviera for a few more days of bathing then drive on to the farm in Tuscany where I wanted to spend the rest of my life. We said goodbye to them both. Raimonde's last words were "Don't leave it another twenty five years before you return."

Monsieur Moulaire added with a smile and a wink: "*Et n'oubliez jamais*, stick peanuts up your arse."

I decide it best to leave that last visit thirty years

ago as the last, with its happy memories. Besides, I want to get to Avignon well before dusk.

The autoroute crosses the rolling hills of Provence. The geology is sharply red with the painter Cezanne's favourite mountain getting bigger by the kilometre. The weather has cleared up but the crosswind is ferocious and America lurches dramatically. We pull into Avignon soon after 2pm.

I'd first come to Avignon on the Friday, just six days after Tigerlily's phone call and warning. I had to get away from those nightmare images playing on every TV station 24/7. This time I'm here to see a special lady.

America and I drive round and round the streets surrounding the medieval walls trying to find the campsite I'd been recommended. After yet another tour of the walls we take a different turn and suddenly I'm driving this large autocaravan through narrow streets inside the walls. This is strictly illegal and I wait to be pulled over by a traffic flic. Somehow we manage to squeeze back out through another gate, or where a gate had once been, and cross the bridge over the river Rhone and pull into the campsite. It's pretty nice, set under tall plane trees and we're allocated a berth. I moor America next to a German camper that looks like it's been here for months.

It's a ten minute walk back across the bridge into the old town. Tonight I'm going to eat at an Indian restaurant I discovered six years ago when I should have been eating Provencal but I chickened out. Tonight too I'm tikka-chickening in.

In the morning I walk across the bridge and

through the town to the bus stop for the TGV station. I want to go to Lyons as the TGV station there was designed by the greatest living Spanish architect Santiago Calatrava. I buy a ticket and the high speed train pulls in.

Whoosh and we're flying across the south of France. This is about as fast as a normal person can travel on Earth without quite taking off. I love the TGVs. We fly through Valence and on to Lyons but the train leaves the fast line and goes through the outskirts of Lyon pulling into the old central station. Bugger. I got the wrong train. I check the schedules and, sure enough, where I should have gone was Lyons airport instead. That's where the spectacular space-age station is. It's too late now as this afternoon I have a date. The next train back to Avignon isn't long coming and I'm back in America just after lunch time.

Around four I walk back across the bridge, through the old stone gate and up the hill to the papal palace, that massive ignoble symbol of Roman Catholic avarice with its fortress walls that once protected those fat, corrupt popes' treasure from greedy outsiders.

I'm looking for a painting of a lady, a special lady, but she's nowhere in the palace as I do such a lightning tour throughout the building I bet tourists think I work there. The thing is I've been before. Twice. The first time was nearly a week after I got that phone call from Tigerlily before the world was turned inside out. The second time was about a year later to take slides of the palace for a new lecture I was preparing on the papacy.

In the gift shop I find some postcards of the lady

I'm looking for and ask the gentleman behind the desk where I can find her. He gives me clear directions: Out into the square, turn right and go straight up the hill to the building at the far wall. It's called The Grand Palace. It's not nearly as grand as the palace I've just left.

I find her on the second floor. I get this unholy kick whenever I see a new Madonna of Mercy for the first time. It's really a variation of trainspotting. She's the last of them on my list and I mentally tick her off.

She's tiny!

The whole painting is fifty centimetres high by forty wide. But she's got all the attributes of her genre put together. She doesn't seem so resigned to her fate as so many images of her do. Conceiving without sinning isn't much fun. She's holding God Jr. in her arms who's looking very smug in his jazzy clothes, holding out his hands, flexing his magical mysterious powers. Angels hold out mum's blue cloak the inside of which is lined with ermine against the cold. Underneath, in its shelter kneel the little people, men to her right, women to her left. A pope, two cardinals and a bishop kneel with the rest of the men and in the foreground the penitents, the flagellants, in their head-to-toe white cassocks with eyeholes cut in their hoods and large circles cut in the cloth on their backs where they've spent serious time whipping themselves so it looks like they've got Neapolitan pizzas pinned to them. The gold leaf background needs some restoration but, all said and done, this is the perfect little Madonna of Mercy, thoroughly stealable. The ladies in uniform in the next room may seem lost in chit chat but they'd be onto me the second I tried to lift the wooden panel off the wall. They don't seem to bother when I photograph her but my flash reflects off the wooden based tempera.

That's my blind date in Avignon. She's the last Lady of Mercy, patroness of justice, charity and hospitals and protectress against the plague, on my long list, and the perfect one to finish off with. I send postcards of her to Ennio in Tuscania and Donatella in Rome.

Next morning I empty America's sewage system, fill up her water tanks. We're going to see the Pont du Gard, the greatest surviving Roman aqueduct.

We set off for Arles. Driving and navigating simultaneously can lead to some lengthy diversions. We get as far as Tarascon (nice castle) when I realise we should have been heading for Alès, not Arles. We turn around and follow the Gardon river valley and turn off at the sign posts for the aqueduct. For one of the top five tourist sites in France the place is empty. But then it is February. I weave America through one car park after another eventually pulling up close to the restaurant and presumably the tourist centre. The only other visitors are two women, one of whom stands behind her parked car. She's removed and is cleaning her dentures.

The aqueduct is massive even when you first see it from quite far away. Up close it is sheer weight. Its nearly fifty metre high columns sit firmly on the rocks of the river bed. I walk across the eighteenth century bridge that runs alongside the lowest and largest of the Roman arches. There's graffiti dating back centuries on the stones of the columns. There's the Roman aqueduct in Segovia to look forward to, still to come. A young couple with their dog are the only other people on the bridge. I stroll through the overcast morning back to America and we head for Nimes.

After trying to get into the once Roman town with its famous temple and other relics, I find we're up a country lane so we give up on Roman ruins and hit the autoroute. My map shows interesting city walls at a town called Carcassonne so that's where we're going when the heavens open and down comes the rain again as we head across the plain towards Spain. With the wind behind us we fly, and we're too heavy to aquaplane.

America and I leave the coast route and climb steadily up into hillier ground with lusher forests than by the coast. We're mates by now, hell bent on escaping together. We're travelling through a hilly landscape that was once Cathar castle country back when Saint Francis was undergoing a change of heart, Venice was about to hijack the Fourth Crusade and later-to-be Saint Dominic, was rooting out Cathar heretics and setting them on fire.

The outskirts of Carcassonne are a concrete jumbletown like most suburbs though they appear marginally better built. I follow road signs for a campsite and pull in just as a lady in a Renault Clio, (THE ladies car,) pulls out. She says the campsite is closed for the winter. I drive around following other signs that say *Cité* and suddenly I can see turrets up on a the rain-swept hill but I keep coming up to this old, low stone bridge that's lower than America.

Finally I give up and drive along a one way street the wrong way hoping any traffic police are indoors sheltering from what is now a fairly good impersonation of a tropical downpour. We climb a steep narrow street that's pretending to be a cataract and doing a fairly good job at it, and emerge at the top and there are the castle walls! On our left like a mirage in a desert that suddenly transmogrified into an oasis, though all the elements were opposites, there's a sign saying *Seulement campers* , ONLY campers!

I do a U-turn and drive America down the steep narrow road for *seulemente* campers and come to a barrier. The toll robot hoarsely barks 5 euros for 24 hours. There're a couple of campers parked under the trees beyond the red and white striped barrier. I dig out a 5 euro note and try to feed it in to the slot indicated, but the driving rain reduces the note to a soggy pulp before it makes it into the slot. I give up screaming, ping America's flashing blinkers, grab the umbrella, jump out and hit the waterfall. Just up the hill is the fortress and outside the main gate, still rotating in the downpour is a fairground roundabout. A child is riding a horse or a dragon. I approach the little decorated cabin where you pay for a ride. Half expecting a rebuff and, pushing my wet 5 euro note under the glass, I ask if the kind *gentilhomme* will give me five coins for it. Lo and behold he does. With a smile too. Vive la France! I wade back to America, slip the coins into the robot, take the ticket it spits out, the striped bar rises and we're in.

I park overlooking the streets and glistening, steep, slate roofs below, on what is a relatively level piece of the space, have a pee outside under my umbrella in the rain, lock America and go off to explore.

The double walled citadel is famous. After Schloss Neuschwanstein in Bavaria, built by mad king Ludwig II with the money given to him by Wilhelm of Prussia to keep out of politics, Cité de Carcassonne is next in line on the prize list for the Walt Disney fairy tale castle stakes. With its double ring wall, conically capped turrets, moat, drawbridge and castle keep, it has nearly everything. Inside the second wall, narrow streets are lined with tourist shops soaking in the winter rain. I find a bar and quaff a beer along with lots of other dripping tourists. A quick umbrella tour later, spoilt for choice, I choose a restaurant and sit at the smallest table and order *paté de fois gras* because it's banned in Chicago, roast duck and a large jug of red wine. Groups of musicians take turns to distract everyone from their food which is unfair on both the food and the music, all a mixture of wild Franco Iberian intoxication.

I staggered back to America in the pouring rain. I have a decision to make tomorrow. I have a second cousin married to a Spaniard and they live in an old water-mill in north central Spain. I could head there or I could go to the south where an English couple live. I met them when they stayed with my Bolsena friends a year ago. I'll toss a coin; heads, right and north west, tails straight on and south.

The next morning I wander the damp empty streets looking for a café. Most shops are closed, missing out on trade as two large groups of Japanese tourists are taking photographs and videoing each other taking photographs and videoing each other crowding the drawbridge. I give up looking for coffee, paddle back to America and we go down through the lower town, out on to the motorway and drive back to Narbonne then on to Perpignan.

It's midday, Sunday, and I'm free. America and I plunge over the border into Spain like escaped POWs in a cheap World War II flick.

Hey Kazim, thanks. You too Astrid. If it wasn't for you two I'd still probably be living in a stone farmhouse on a hillside in eastern Tuscany with a view out over the upper Tiber valley and the Mountains of the Moon beyond. If you hadn't seduced me Astrid (and it wasn't difficult was it? I wasn't exactly hard to get) and then dumped me for Kazim, I'd still be mowing grass, slashing back brambles, tugging up stinking wild elder roots, wasting my life irrigating flowers, worrying about the leaking roof, the cobwebs or the dirty windows, or the million and one other jobs that needed doing from which there was no rest unless you drank enough cheap wine to be capable of tackling any of them yet still realising that you're incapable. If you hadn't persuaded Big Pete to go back to Perugia and give Kazim that face lift Astrid, I'd still be mentally waking up in the middle of the nightmare to the roar of a late summer forest fire or the rumbling of falling masonry as the earthquake finally brings down the bulging southern wall that had withstood everything since 1776, the date inscribed into the stone lintel over the small western bedroom window with the sevens back-to-front. If you hadn't gone back to him and we hadn't come and forcefully removed you from him before he exacted his revenge for your spray painting his face black and kicking him in the balls as Big Pete worked on him with his cutter, I wouldn't be rolling along in America with everything I own sitting right beside and behind me, not knowing what new scene I'm going to wake up to the next day, who I'm going to meet and what I'm going to learn. So, Astrid, as you work to become a doctor and get better at being a single mom and a winner, and you Kazim, whatever you're up to, maybe getting better at being a loser and getting used to the idea that you're not going to get any more money out of me, thank you both. You changed my life, both of you. If it hadn't been for you both I'd never have done this and I'm so appreciative that you did it when you did so that I can still do what I'm doing while I can still do it. You made the youth of my old age.

And Kazim, hey! Look on the bright side. We all got to win something out of this; you, me and Astrid.

You got your Italian papers. You're a legal citizen thanks to me and my mates. And you got ten grand. That's more money than you ever had before. Your scar is going to pull birds galore. You can even invent any amount of stories as to how you got that swipe down your cheek. They'll love it. Go for it. I'll even make some up for you if you're stuck for a tale or two and they needn't include a man called Peter Ramsbottom.

Astrid got back to the States and after some wobbly years of ups and downs she's finally settled into advanced education and on her way to a doctorate and a useful and rewarding career.

I'm free. And I'll get to write this book.

Oh, and thank you Mother of Mercy. I'm not too sure exactly what you did but you did something in all that mish mash and plif plaf. I'm still an atheist and believe I always will be but I have a healthy respect for what you can do when you put your heart into it. Also you're a fabulous icon. It was great having the time to get to know you better.

America and I climb the hill going west. There's very little traffic. I'm sad I've left one of the most beautiful countries in the world but, thirty one years in paradise in one lifetime isn't bad. *Paradiso sulla terra*. Now we're moving on. Now it's high time for new faces, new feelings, new names, new scenes, new sounds, new tastes and new words.

I brain mail thank you messages to Michelangela and Ellie for doing so much to help me get this far. I wonder if I'll ever see them again. I hope so. Maybe they'll come and visit me if I get extradited from Spain and flung into an Italian slammer for writing all this stuff. That's when Scarface and his pals would come and visit me too. I godda keep rollin'.

There's that important decision coming up; one of those life-changing decisions that you look back on and wonder what if? Very soon I have to choose between turning right and heading north west to La Rioja or going straight on south to Murcia. The older I get the better I used to be at this sort of thing. I used to have a mantra for decision making: it's either or, or neither. Sometimes I would flip it to a variation: it's neither nor, nor either. Whatever which way I juggled it, I always ended up tossing a coin or whatever. I thought of doing that last night in Carcassonne, but somehow, with all that red wine and rain, I never did.

In the end it's America that seems to make the decision. At the crucial crossroads she just keeps going straight ahead.

Epilogue

Once America and I got off the *autovia* E15, the first person I saw in Spain was a hooker! She stood at a roundabout with her blonde hair, short blue dress and high heels. She perked up when I imagined she saw her late luncheon voucher, a single man driving a camper van, coming round the bend towards her. I pretended I had a wife and kids safely stowed away in the back playing Trivial Pursuits and our happy family swerved passed her and kept on going towards Barcelona.

America and I ended up in the southern Spanish region of Murcia beside the Mar Menor, one of the largest salt lakes in the Mediterranean. English friends of English friends in Italy steered me towards a campsite right on the beach and generally helped me find my feet. I enrolled into an intensive Spanish language programme. I knew they said *hallo* backwards but I went on to learn Spanish isn't just Italian with a lisp minus a syllable or two. Oil (as in olive oil), *aciete* in Spanish sounds just like vinegar, *aceto,* in Italian. *Azafata* (hostess), well that just sounds Arabic. Whereas in Italian you say appreciatively *una bellissima donna*, in Spanish you'd say *una chica guapa* which to me sounded glib until I learnt the Spanish word for heart is *corazon.*

As I read about Spanish history and the still open wounds of their civil war, surprisingly, I re-discovered Englishness. I'd lived for over forty years outside the country of my birth and here were the dialects, the foods, the attitudes and opinions I had to catch up with.

America's Italian documents expired one by one over a period of weeks. At some point I almost felt I was going to have to abandon the camper van that had used no engine oil (*aciete*) in the 2,000 kilometer journey from central Italy, in a corner of the campsite next to other rusting hulks where it would become a home to stray cats, forgotten dreams and sparrows. We were caught in a Catch 22: Couldn't get insurance without an ITV (the Spanish road test certificate) and no ITV without insurance!

I put it all on a back burner in June when I flew to Los Angeles where my daughter, the year before, had married her tall, dark, handsome Texan. He'd phoned me in Italy months earlier to ask for her hand in marriage which was totally unexpected as I didn't think people did that any more. They were married in a civil ceremony in Santa Barbara and six months later planned the summer festival for families and friends on a hilltop north of Malibu. On the eve of that summer's blue moon, as the sun dipped below the western hills, the bride, looking radiantly happy in a golden dress and heavily pregnant, walked down the grassy aisle between the rows of seated guests as a musician played 'Here comes the Bride' with a cello bow on a logger's saw. She and the groom were re-married under a white parasol in a flower bedecked wooden rowing boat by Captain Hank, a retired naval officer in full dress uniform, qualified for the job provided there was a crew of less than six.

In August my father died and in September my daughter gave birth to a healthy baby girl with "a head of black hair, deep blue eyes, long, long fingers, and a vice-like grip."

Back in Murcia, a good Spanish legal firm got America's documents in order even though it took a bit of illegal driving at *siesta* time when I thought the *guardia* would most likely be recovering from their lunch. By early spring of 2008, America and I were back on the road.

As the Italian, American and British media reported from the frescoed medieval courthouse on the sensational case of drugs, sex and murder among young foreigners in the capitol city of the "Green Heart of Italy", way across on the other side of the planet, about as far away from all of that as it's possible to get, Astrid was awarded her PhD and became a doctor.

Claouey, France, 2008.